Literary Trails

Haworth and the Brontës

Literary Trails
Haworth and the Brontës

Catherine Rayner and David Walford

PEN & SWORD
HISTORY

AN IMPRINT OF PEN & SWORD BOOKS LTD.
YORKSHIRE - PHILADELPHIA

First published in Great Britain in 2018 by
PEN AND SWORD HISTORY
an imprint of
Pen & Sword Books Ltd
Yorkshire - Philadelphia

ISBN 978 1 52672 085 6

Typeset in Ehrhardt 11/15 by
Aura Technology and Software Services, India
Printed and bound in India by Replika Press Pvt. Ltd.

Pen & Sword Books Ltd incorporates the Imprints of Pen & Sword Books
Archaeology, Atlas, Aviation, Battleground, Discovery, Family History,
History, Maritime, Military, Naval, Politics, Railways, Select, Transport,
True Crime, Fiction, Frontline Books, Leo Cooper, Praetorian Press,
Seaforth Publishing, Wharncliffe and White Owl.

For a complete list of Pen & Sword titles please contact

PEN & SWORD BOOKS LIMITED
47 Church Street, Barnsley, South Yorkshire, S70 2AS, England
E-mail: enquiries@pen-and-sword.co.uk
Website: www.pen-and-sword.co.uk

or

PEN AND SWORD BOOKS
1950 Lawrence Rd, Havertown, PA 19083, USA
E-mail: Uspen-and-sword@casematepublishers.com

Contents

Authors' Acknowledgements

Many people must work together to produce a book and in this task I have had the company and expertise of my brother David who has walked and written about many Yorkshire routes. I have an abiding interest in the Brontë family and their writings, am a Life Member of the Brontë Society and have served on its Board of Trustees for some years. I am grateful to the staff of Pen and Sword Books Ltd for giving us both the opportunity to pool our specialities and produce a book that will serve the social historian, the walker and all those with a literary interest in the Brontë family. I must further acknowledge the many researchers and writers who have studied the lives and works of the Brontë family and the area in which they lived. Of these I am especially grateful to Dr Juliet Barker, Philip Lister, S. R. Whitehead and Steven Wood and the continuing support of the staff of the Brontë Parsonage Museum.

Catherine Rayner,
Nafferton, East Yorkshire.

This has been an interesting and inspiring project for which I am indebted to my sister Catherine, as I have become enveloped by the fascinating history of the remarkable Brontë family and their lives in and around Haworth. I also acknowledge the work of groups and individuals who have worked over many years to establish several long-distance footpaths across this part of Yorkshire. This is an inspiring part of Britain to take to the open air, as we try to link 200 years of history, to enrich your walks in the countryside of West Yorkshire.

David F. Walford,
Bainton, East Yorkshire.

Also by the same authors

Catherine Rayner:

'Wild Imaginings': A Brontë Childhood
The Brontë Sisters: Life, Loss and Literature

David F. Walford:

Yorkshire Wolds Wanderings
Yorkshire Railway Rambles, Volume One: North and East Yorkshire
Yorkshire Wolds Wanderings, Revised Second Edition
It Was To Be The Big One

List of Maps

All photographs in this book are by
David F Walford, unless stated otherwise.

All maps in this book are taken from Open Street Maps,
with modifications by the authors.

Chapter 1

Introduction

Through the pages of this book, we wish to guide you along a series of journeys: on foot, or possibly by cycle or horseback, in groups or alone to take you back in time by almost two centuries to the town of Haworth in West Yorkshire and over its surrounding moorlands.

This exceptional part of Yorkshire greatly inspired the remarkable Brontë sisters to write their beautiful poetry and seven extraordinary novels. Their home and environment affected their lives and imaginations and prompted an enormous outpouring of juvenile writings, letters, poetry and books which are imbued with their surroundings, the weather and the beauty of the countryside at a time when the rural way of life was being eroded.

West Yorkshire experienced great changes in the early years of the nineteenth century as the impact of the industrial revolution was felt across the northern part of England. In just a few years the way of life – along with the landscape – changed dramatically. Industry, not agriculture, would be the way ahead for the majority of the population. Haworth was a major part of this revolution.

The Reverend Patrick Brontë, incumbent of St Michael and All Angels church at Haworth, (1820–61) strove to minister to the thousands of mill workers, employed in the new textile industries and a large and disseminated congregation of farmers, quarrymen, home workers and miners. Many were poor and had large families to raise. The economic and industrial changes caused upheaval and discontent, including the questioning of religion and doubting of faith in the Christian church. The Haworth community included many dissenters from the Protestant religion alongside pagan and atheist practices. The Rev. Brontë had an enormous job to try to keep the community stable and healthy in these revolutionary times.

The Parsonage at Haworth stands at just under 250 metres above sea level, (800ft). Slightly closer to the Irish Sea than the North Sea, Haworth is just to the east of the Pennine Way long distance footpath. The M62 east–west motorway, built in the 1960s, is eighteen kilometres (eleven miles), to the south. Linking the Mersey to the Humber, the motorway leaves Liverpool and by-passes Manchester before climbing over the Pennine Hills towards Halifax, then Leeds and eventually reaching the outskirts of Hull.

To the north, the main Airedale corridor of river, rail and road forms the route south-east to Bradford and Leeds. To the north-west is Skipton, then on to Kendal to the west and Carlisle to the north. The famous Settle–Carlisle railway (1847) still carries passengers along this dramatic route, with all trains stopping at Keighley. It is at this location that the preserved Keighley and Worth Valley Railway takes a southerly route, south to Haworth and Oxenhope.

Although this railway opened after the deaths of the Brontë sisters, we cover the history and connecting walks along this interesting route. Through the hard work of the volunteers, it forms an ideal means of absorbing the historical background of the area, as steam locomotives labour up and down the heavily graded line, pulling their rolling stock, with thousands of visitors to the towns.

The Brontë sisters made use of the new form of transport, and from 1847 were able to take trains at Keighley to travel down to London along with several visits to York and the Yorkshire coast. Charlotte also travelled to Scotland, Cumbria and Ireland. The Brontë sisters invested some of their inheritance from their aunt into railway shares and Branwell worked for a time as a railway clerk.

We aim to help you to wander around Haworth and over the moors, as you visualise the scene in the first half of the nineteenth century. We will help you to walk along the same paths as Anne, Emily and Charlotte Brontë and to be inspired by their words and verse, as you experience the unique atmosphere of the moors and the narrow streets and ancient buildings of the West Yorkshire town. This is Brontë Country: wild, dramatic, exhilarating and steeped in centuries of social history, conflict, hardship, love, legend, mystery and drama.

Above: An ancient boundary stone high on Haworth Moor, surrounded by heather and common cotton sedge, which both grow on peat and acid soils of heath and moorland.

Below: View looking south down Main Street, Haworth, from the cobbled square at the top of the hill.

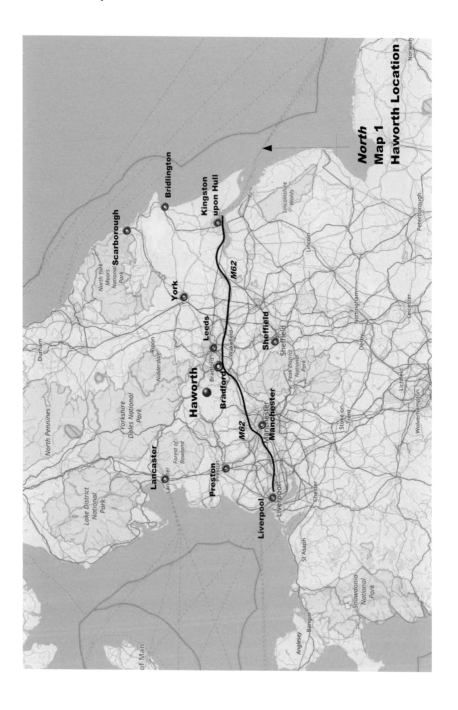

North
Map 1
Haworth Location

Chapter 2

West Yorkshire and the Haworth area

'Out on a wild and windy moor'
Kate Bush, 1978

There can surely be few more stunning, yet barren areas of moorland that can invoke and inspire such dramatic scenes and lyrics as captured by Emily Brontë and appreciated by all manner of artists ever since. These are the moors above and beyond Haworth spreading for miles to the west and containing old farmsteads and ruined houses dating back to the Elizabethan era and where people have lived and worked for centuries. They can be covered in swirling mist or blazing sunshine, snow and piercing gales, or have an eerie calm. They can be loud with the cries of animals and birds or silent as a tomb in their deep holes and clefts. They are harsh and they are beautiful.

The moors make up an amazing area that is now known as Brontë Country and through the pages of this book, we wish to guide you on a journey over and around this exceptional part of Yorkshire. Your journey will reveal what helped to inspire the Brontë sisters who became three of the most famous and respected of English authors, and why it created a worldwide interest in their lives and works.

This book is a guide to the immediate area in and around Haworth, where the remarkable Brontë siblings played, walked, were educated, worshipped and wrote. We will trace many of the walks they undertook so many times in the early decades of the nineteenth century.

Haworth at that time was a flourishing mill town which developed quickly in the race to bring large-scale mechanical production into the wool, cotton and linen industries. It was blessed with plentiful soft water supplies and, prior to the development of the steam engine, this would have been used not only to wash the wool, but also to power the waterwheels, which in turn powered the large looms and other machinery in the textile mills.

Haworth is a town six kilometres (four miles), south of Keighley, around thirteen kilometres (eight miles), west of Bradford and sixteen kilometres (ten miles) north of Halifax. It is so easy to have a romantic view of such places in the early part of the twenty-first century but many of our now treasured locations around the country mask a very dark industrial past that would have made life for those living through it difficult and often very short.

Many small villages became hives of activity within just a generation as the effects of industrialisation spread. Although the full impact of the industrial revolution had to wait until the development of the railway network, locations like Haworth became a natural magnet for textile mills because it had all the necessary raw materials: the plentiful supply of clean water, hundreds of sheep grazing over the local moors, some seams of coal and plenty of stone for building materials.

Without coal, fire could only be created by using wood, peat, or a very limited supply of expensive oil. Transport was appalling, but then it had been since the Romans had left our shores in the 5th Century AD. There remained a few pack horse trails, and many turnpike toll roads, but nothing that could move large quantities of goods quickly, unless you had access to navigable waters. Travel was difficult, slow, uncomfortable and principally for the more wealthy. The cost and speed of moving goods greatly limited trade.

Most settlements in the Yorkshire area had their own quarries, woodlands for fuel, water supplies and food production. If an area was fortunate, there may be supplies of coal available in open-cast mines or shallow drifts into the sides of the hills. Peat was another possible source of fuel, though it would not produce a roaring fire.

A principle network of 'mail routes' started to improve some elements of long distance travel, through the latter years of the eighteenth century, though this had minimal impact on the movement of goods. The first canals were also to be seen in the later years of that century, but it is important to put the canals into context. They did provide an improvement to the movement of goods, but the network was limited, expensive and slow to build. It should also be remembered that a canal boat would do well to achieve an average of 2mph, for up to twelve hours per day. Pulled by a horse and continually delayed at locks, where queues of vessels would form at busy times, passage was very slow. At some locations of multiple locks, a full day may be lost, waiting to pass laboriously through each level. Added to this was the arduous procedures for loading and discharging cargoes, all creating further interruptions. The 'golden age' of canal transport, can be a misleading concept. They did make a positive impact on some industries but growth was limited. Most canals generally link navigable waterways. Undulating ground was most unsuitable for this form of construction and the expense of locks made it often prohibitory.

As a consequence of these travel difficulties, a location like Haworth was ideal for industry. It had fast running water to power the mill wheels and wash the products and building materials were to hand. Raw materials did not need to be moved long distances and a workforce would always move to where the work was. The district in and around Haworth, like many northern towns, became the location for dozens of mills, powered at first by waterwheels and later by steam.

The current picture-postcard town of Haworth would have been enveloped with smoke and filth, along with the detritus of thousands of people in a town with no appropriate sanitation. Many of the poorer people lived in squalor, and disease was rife in the tightly packed terraced houses which were often built just a few metres from the mills that provided their tenants' employment. Life expectancy was short and averaged only twenty-five years. Infant mortality was amongst the highest in the country and a visit to the churchyard adjoining the Parsonage visibly expresses these facts.

As most historians will recognise, few locations illustrate the history of a community more than the parish church and the graveyard. The size of a community can be demonstrated by the alterations, building and rebuilding of the churches and chapels. It also indicates the wealth as local benefactors would often fund improvements. The church records and graveyard would indicate where disease or a change of employment may have led to a long term reduction in the population. Each headstone tells its own story; death in infancy, death in childhood or in the workplace, a spate of deaths through epidemics such as smallpox, diphtheria, pneumonia, cholera, and tuberculosis decimated the population repeatedly and yet a continuing high birth rate often balanced the losses.

Haworth was no exception. Never have we viewed a graveyard such as that between the church and the Parsonage at Haworth; no neat, well-spaced rows of headstones to slowly walk between. The graveyard at Haworth resembles a football crowd with thousands of headstones separated only by yet more stones laid flat, all highlighting the overwhelming impact of so many deaths. This location still cannot fail to stun the onlooker, over 150 years after its closure on public health grounds. Through hard and dangerous work, squalid living conditions, polluted water supplies, poor sanitation and disease, the town of Haworth was killing its own community in the nineteenth century.

Into this town in the new age of industrialisation, the Reverend Patrick Brontë brought his young wife and children to Haworth

Parsonage in April 1820. It was to be their home for over forty years, until Patrick's death in June 1861, having outlived his entire family. During this time he endured the loss of his young wife, just over a year after they came to Haworth, and then of his two eldest daughters aged only 11 and 10 years old. Tragically, he suffered the loss of all of his six children and their aunt, who looked after them after the death of their mother. It is testament to the man's staunch beliefs and courage that he kept his faith throughout a life which took so much and so many away from him, yet he always found time to help and comfort others.

As we guide you along our selection of walks, we will try to help you to visualise life in those early years of the nineteenth century. We will point out the many remains of ruined farmsteads dotted around the moors. We will highlight the empty stone quarries and their overgrown tracks over which the materials moved and the workforce would trek every day. We will show the few mill chimneys that remain and we will help you to visualise and multiply them by many dozens. Each would belch forth clouds of thick smoke leaving a toxic dirty smog over the town and surrounding countryside. Instead of motor vehicles, the sound of horses struggling up the steep narrow streets would reverberate whilst heavy textile mill machinery clattered and clanked throughout much of the day and into the night.

Later in the century, a constant reminder of railway power would emerge with locomotive whistles shrieking, huge pistons labouring at the head of a heavy train, the clinking of loose-coupled trucks as their buffers repeatedly collided with those of its neighbour. This would all add to the general noise and smoke as each train struggled with the gradients. The industrial revolution came early to Haworth, as it did to many of the mill towns of Yorkshire and Lancashire and life was changing very rapidly when the Brontë family took up their residence there.

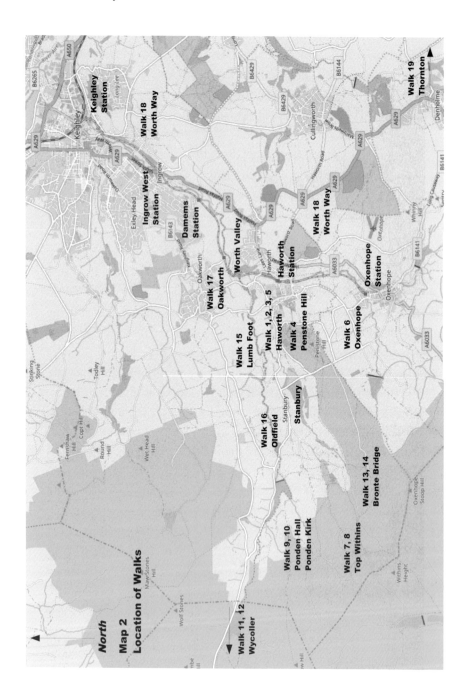

Above: Vale Mill today with the railway track running beside it. One of the only remaining mills of the twenty or more that surrounded Haworth in the 19th Century.

Below: Looking East from Haworth station platform towards the last remnant of Ebor Mill, its chimney.

Chapter 3

A guide to safe and responsible walking

Many visitors to the area will just wish to take a stroll around the quaint cobbled streets of Haworth, maybe take in a visit to the Parsonage and a tea shop or two, along the Main Street. Through the pages of this book we wish to help your thoughts to wander back in time and experience this town through the eyes of its famous inhabitants. We will lead you out onto the moors where the Brontë children were free to let their bodies and imaginations grow. This is an exciting area with an amazing history and you can become involved and entertained within this unique part of our social and literary heritage

Before you take to your walking boots, it is important that when you leave the confines of your transport you are aware of the following guidelines. Many of you may well be familiar with what follows but for the novice it is important to know as much as possible about the rights and responsibilities required to walk safely.

Much of this part of Yorkshire (including the moors) is farmed. The ecology is fragile on the moors, whilst areas around the town may be more intensively cultivated. Livestock grazes, an abundance of wildlife thrives, watercourses flow and many local people live and work here. Please follow these simple guidelines and respect the area, so that they may be safely enjoyed and lived in by many more generations to come.

Follow all aspects of the Country Code. In particular, keep to public rights of way and respect the terms of open access land. If you take your dog it must be kept under control at all times. If your dog is well behaved, you may not feel it necessary to keep it on a lead but please understand that sheep will panic at the sight of a running dog. If they are carrying lambs, great damage can be done. The young lambs may also bolt away and lose their mother in the confusion.

What appears to be an empty moor is almost certainly the home of many ground-nesting birds. An excited dog may crush the eggs or chicks, whilst creating panic to the parent birds. Always keep your dog on a lead, please!

Have a few plastic bags with you so that any litter, or dog waste, may be collected and disposed of appropriately. If you find a gate closed, please check after you and all of your party has passed through, that it is securely shut and fastened by the last person. Unattended farm machinery may look very interesting to children but do not let them tamper with it. It could be the cause of a serious injury. If you are on cycle or horseback, understand the difference between footpaths and bridleways (see details in map reading section) and avoid causing yourself, as well as other people, inconvenience and difficulties.

All the maps in this book are intended as a general guide only and every attempt is made to ensure that the information is correct at the time of going to press. Always please take note of any footpath diversion instructions that are made from time to time, or restrictions on open access land. If in doubt, refer to the Ordnance Survey maps.

The paths and tracks marked on the maps contained in this book are no absolute guarantee of the existence of a public right of way. Many have been recorded from personal knowledge but all have been ascertained by thorough research at the time of going to print. Please note that some private roads are only marked to assist you to identify your exact location. If you are in any doubt about a right of way you can contact your local council definitive rights of way officer, who will have the most up to date information.

Public rights of way are generally quite well signposted, though sometimes markers may be missing so it is always advisable to have the appropriate Ordnance Survey map with you. The numbers of the Landranger Series of OS maps that cover this area are: 103 and

104. Map 103 covers the area to the west of Haworth and as far as Blackburn and Clitheroe. Map 104 covers Haworth and the area to the east, including Bradford and Leeds. The OS Landranger Series are the most commonly used, being an all-purpose map, with a scale of 1:50,000 (1.25 inches to the mile).

For more detailed maps at a scale of 1:25,000 (2.50 inches to the mile), seek out the Explorer Series, (also known as the Pathfinder Series or the Outdoor Leisure maps). The numbers are: OL 21, OL 288 and OL 297. Map OL 21 covers Haworth and the areas to the north, west and south. Explorer map 288, or OL 288, covers the area east of Haworth, including Bradford and Huddersfield. Explorer map 297 (OL 297) is the area to the north east of Haworth and across to Harrogate.

For the keen walker and cyclist, the Explorer Series of maps has been particularly designed to appeal to the outdoor enthusiast and includes extensive tourist information. Footpaths are clearly marked, along with field boundaries, making navigation easier. See the diagram to aid you to identify the maps you need for your journey. If you are a regular walker, we strongly recommend you to make an investment in a good set of maps. They will aid your enjoyment of an area whilst providing a continuing reference guide throughout your walks. With the exception of Walk 19, (the Thornton town trail), every walk in this book is on the area covered by the OS Outdoor Leisure map number OL 21, at a scale of 1:25,000

Detailed maps will help you to understand the different types of public highways across our countryside. It is important to remember that even a footpath is termed as a highway! Footpaths, Bridleways, Green Lanes, and Permissive Footpath/Bridleway are all highways. By simple definition, you can walk on a footpath and it will be around 1.2m to 1.5 metres wide, (4ft). You cannot use your bike on a footpath. A Bridleway is open to walkers, cyclists and horse riders. It is usually 3m wide and will have gates instead of styles or kissing gates, to cross fenced boundaries. A track or Green Lane is technically open to all forms of transport. It has the same access as a fully surfaced highway but should be treated with the utmost respect. In recent years the advent of the four-wheeled-drive vehicle has become a fashionable, off-road form of leisure. These machines can create terrible damage to the delicate nature of the countryside if used carelessly. These ancient Green Lanes were created in an age when the most powerful land transport was a horse, so they are fragile.

Open Access land is a relatively new concept and many such areas were created a decade ago, to improve access to special areas of the countryside where intensive farming methods were generally not used; grazing land, open moors and some wetlands. There may be restrictions placed on such areas to permit the recovery of plants and grassland. There may be other requirements for restricted access such as: breeding seasons, maintenance work, drainage projects. Most land is still under private ownership and possibly an important means of income to local farmers. Please respect the areas and adhere to any restrictions placed at certain times of the year.

If you are unfamiliar with map reading, these few tips should help. Maps nearly always position north at the top, (as is the case with all maps in this book), if possible face north yourself to read the map when you are on your rambles. If you are unsure which direction you are facing, then use a compass to establish north and face that way. A further guide comes from the sun. At midday, it will be to the south, so stand with your back to it to face north.

View the surrounding countryside with the maps set out in front of you to get your 'bearings' and a feel for the area. For example, pinpoint a landmark, such as a church tower or a mill chimney, on the map. Then locate the same structure in the landscape. Likewise, if you are standing next to a farm building with a lane going off to the right, (east), find the position on the map, then trace the route of the track out to the east. After studying a few views with the map in your hands, you will soon learn how to identify your location and the surrounding landscape. Practical use such as this is the most effective way to learn how to read a map.

In this book, all distances are in metric, (metres and kilometres). If you are more at home with imperial measurements, remember a few simple conversions to help you. One metre is 3.2808ft, so a quick conversion is one metre to just over 3ft. One kilometre is 0.625 miles, thus eight kilometres are equal to five miles. As a further help the grid lines on the OS maps divide the countryside into one square kilometre areas, thereby giving a quick guide to the distance between two places by counting the number of grid lines crossed.

Another useful skill is to learn how to take a grid reference. At the bottom of the key on all OS maps, a simple example is given how to find any location on a map by using a six-number grid reference. Remember the 'Easting' comes first and are read horizontally along the bottom of the map. The 'Northing' second, read vertically up the side of the map. In this book, a grid reference number is quoted in the 'Fact File' accompanying each walk, giving the exact start and finish location.

If you have the misfortune to have an accident in the countryside, giving the emergency services a grid reference for the casualty may save vital minutes in a rescue situation, when you are not familiar with road names, place names and post codes, or you are in a bleak moorland area. Keep testing yourself and your friends. It is a simple system to learn but can be a very important one.

You will soon get a feel for the distances and the type of terrain: flat, gentle slopes, very steep grassy climb, sudden drop at a cliff, etc. If you want to progress to backpacking in the more remote areas of the country, the ability to read maps accurately is essential. This type of simple exercise is ideal to build your skills and confidence.

Depending what scale of map you are using, contour lines follow a consistent height over your map. These will be at every 50 metres on the 1:50,000 scale Landranger Maps and at 25 metres on the 1:25,000 scale Explorer Maps. Again, regular use of the maps outdoors will improve your skills, as to the type of terrain. Many contour lines bunched closely together indicates a rapid change in altitude, so a steep hill or cliff. Fewer and widely spaced contour lines indicates a flat terrain.

Much is made of modern technology with satellite-navigation systems and a multitude of 'Apps' available on the most basic of phones. All these systems can naturally be of great assistance to follow a route, or to find your exact location, but, and it is a very important but, on moorland and amongst hills it can be very easy to lose your signal. What do you do if your batteries run flat or if you drop your phone into a puddle? If you are going any distance from a main road we would always urge you to have the backup from a good quality map and know how to read it. This is a skill for life.

We are not going to go into details of telling you how to dress but, even for a short walk, it is always wise to be suitably clothed. A stout pair of walking shoes or boots along with a waterproof coat, are really the minimum essentials. If walking a good distance, two pairs of socks cushion the feet and help to prevent blisters. Avoid nylon material, choose more breathable textiles such as cotton or wool. Use a rucksack rather than a hand-held bag to carry your belongings safely. Always have the local OS map and if out on the moors, it is always a good idea to have a compass, whistle, some spare clothes and food. This is one time that you do not need to feel guilty about having a few chocolate bars, or have some fruit to hand. Take a phone, but remember: the signal may be very poor or non-existent, so do not rely solely on this form of communication.

This may sound rather obvious but a particular hazard to walkers in the Yorkshire Dales are wet slabs of stone and cobbled streets. With many centuries of shoes and boots wearing into the surface, the stone slabs and cobbles become extremely smooth. In wet weather they are very slippery, so take extra care, especially when descending a steep slope in the wet. Haworth, Church Street and Main Street are a particular case in point!

If you are tackling some of the routes on your bike, be sure to wear the correct cycling gear, including helmet. Always wear a bright-coloured jacket or high-vis top and have bright panniers at the back, so that you really stand out to traffic behind you. Remember that footpaths are not a right of way for cycles, look out for Bridleways or Green Lanes if you are off-road.

All the routes in this book are generally within a 10 kilometre radius of Haworth as we follow the regular paths used by the Brontë sisters. Several car parks are now located around the town, along with some off-street parking, but please show respect for local residents and businesses. These can become overwhelmed by visitor numbers in the summer months and at the weekends. If parking on country lanes, remember that sizeable farm machinery may need to manoeuvre passed your vehicle whilst you are out on the moors.

This is a great area to enjoy and with a bit of thought and consideration, everyone can help to preserve it. If you want to learn more about map reading or taking compass bearings, then there are plenty of detailed publications available. We strongly recommend you to spend a little time just studying your map when out in the countryside. As mentioned earlier, test yourself by looking at features in the landscape then find them on the map and vice-versa.

We would also urge you to find your own routes when you have gained confidence. Don't just follow the crowd. We will give you enough general information about each area to enable you to customise your route to suit you and your situation. Depending on the weather, and the party of walkers with whom you may be travelling, it is always a good idea to plan for the need to shorten the route if that becomes necessary.

If you are walking over the moors on your own it is always wise to inform someone of your plans. Tell them of your expected route and an approximate time when you expect to return. In the event of anything going wrong at least the alarm will be raised and the general area you are in can be given to the emergency services. Although all these walks are within close proximity to urban centres, even on a clear day it is possible to lose your bearings on the upper part of the moors, so regular checks on your map to identify your location is wise. Whilst all moorland and open countryside is a pleasure to ramble across, it has a history and may contain hidden holes, springs, wells, mineshafts, quarry workings, animal burrows etc.

A day's ramble does not have to be a route march with military precision. Good planning is always wise but the key thing is to enjoy your day out. If you are not a regular walker, start off with short walks to build up your knowledge and stamina. Collect equipment as you increase your distance range. Rambling should be fun, in all types of weather, so be sensible and enjoy your walk.

A collection of essential equipment for walkers including; a small rucksack, light waterproof coat, large scale OS Maps (or similar publications) Map carrying case, compass, whistle, water-bottle, survival bag or blanket, selection of high energy chocolate bars or fruit. You can take a mobile phone but do not rely on receiving a signal. The moors can be a dangerous place at times.

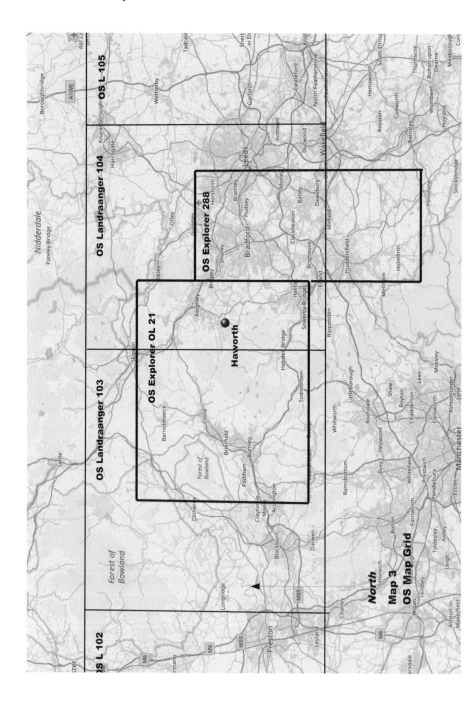

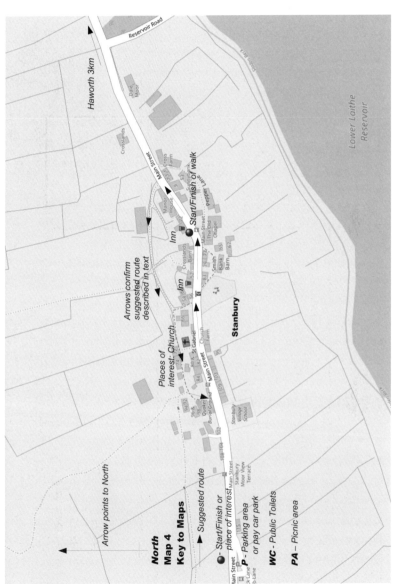

With all the walks we produce a guide map similar to the above, to help you to trace your route on to a detailed OS map, or comparable publication. Spend time looking at the detailed maps of the area you chose to walk and identify the many options to alter your route, if and when necessary.

Chapter 4

The Brontë family: a brief history

If you are using this book for walks in and around Haworth or just for information or have an interest in the area, it is both useful and fascinating to learn a little about the literary family who made this town and its surrounding moorlands so famous.

When the Reverend Patrick Brontë brought his wife and six small children to Haworth in the spring of 1820 they moved into the house that is now the Brontë Parsonage Museum. It is interesting to know how this young family of six children came to Haworth and what influenced their parents.

Patrick Brontë was born in Northern Ireland on St Patrick's Day, 17 March 1777, in the tiny village of Emdale, in the parish of Drumballyroney, County Down. He was the eldest of ten children and was born in a two-roomed thatched cabin with an earth floor. His father, Hugh Brunty or Prunty, was a peasant labourer.

Despite these humble beginnings, Patrick showed flare and intelligence and was an avid reader whenever he could find books. His main two influences were *The Bible* and John Bunyan's, *The Pilgrim's Progress*. Mainly self-educated, the young Patrick worked as both an assistant to a local blacksmith and later a draper, helping with the weaving of the cloth.

By the time he reached 16 years of age, Patrick had enough knowledge and ability to take over a room at the nearby village school and provide local farm children with the rudiments of education. He continued in this work for nearly five years when he was invited by the local rector, the wealthy Thomas Tighe, to tutor his son. Rev. Tighe recognised Patrick's drive and enthusiasm and began to assist him in the study of theology, persuading him to take this up as a career. Patrick had interests in military history, nature and international affairs and had read widely during his teaching years. With Tighe's assistance he also learnt Latin and Greek, at which he excelled.

Patrick, with a small amount of money and a burning ambition to study at Cambridge University, (where Tighe had been a student), sailed to England in September 1802, and took up his place as a sizar (a poor but assisted student) at St John's College, Cambridge. He signed his name in the register as Patrick Brontë, possibly in recognition of his new life and also in honour of his hero, Lord Nelson, recently given the title, The Duke of Brontë. It is a measure of Patrick's hard work and determination that this ambitious young man spent four years at the prestigious university and gained his Batchelor of Arts degree. He was ordained in Holy Orders in August 1806 and took up his first work as a curate at Weathersfield, in Essex.

Under the guidance of the Rev. Tighe, Patrick had been influenced by the Evangelical movement. This was part of the Protestant Church and had been mainly introduced by the Methodist brothers, John and Charles Wesley and members of the Moravian church. Evangelicalism was a belief in four main religious tenets.

These were the ideas that people could repent and be 'born again' in God's grace, that sins would be forgiven and the sinner united with God in Heaven, that the Bible was to be believed and revered as the word of God and that people should actively promote the teachings of the Bible in speech and the written word. Patrick saw part of his role as educating people through preaching and writing and he began to write didactic poetry, sermons and essays to be printed and shared amongst his parishioners.

During the next few years Patrick moved to various parishes and gained more friends and experience. At Wellington, in Shropshire, he met two men who would have a profound influence on his life, the Rev. William Morgan, a cheerful Welshman who also had evangelical leanings and literary ambitions, and John Fennell who was the head of the local school and another follower of Methodism and the Wesley brothers.

Patrick moved to Dewsbury in Yorkshire in 1809 and then on to the village of Hartshead, in 1811. It was around this time that the Luddite riots were taking place in parts of the north of England. Patrick was caught up in some of the unrest in Yorkshire and, whilst he always stood by the law, he had sympathy for the plight of the labourers whose jobs were in jeopardy.

William Morgan was now a curate in Bradford and John Fennell was appointed as the headmaster of the newly opened Wesleyan Academy for the sons of ministers at Woodhouse Grove School, Apperley Bridge, near Bradford, in January 1812. This appointment would bring Patrick and his future wife together.

Maria Branwell, the woman would become Mrs Brontë, was born on 15 April 1783, in Penzance, Cornwall. She was the fifth of eleven children born to wealthy merchant Thomas Branwell and his wife Anne. Maria's upbringing was very different to Patrick's. She was raised as an educated and respected young lady with all the attributes and privileges of her class. She was not expected to work but kept occupied with her education and her household duties and a social round of visiting friends and family. The Branwells had strong Protestant beliefs incorporating Methodism with possibly some Calvinistic ideas. Maria was the model of sobriety and feminine charm with strict moral ideas and behaviour. She led the life of a genteel, middle-class woman of impeccable background and taste.

In 1812, and at the age of 29, Maria arrived at Woodhouse Grove School on a visit to her uncle, by marriage, John Fennell. John had married Maria's cousin, Jane Branwell. The Branwell's business interests in Cornwall were failing and Maria may have intended staying with her relatives to assist at the school. Patrick had been invited to work there, on occasion, to examine the boys in their classical education.

The attraction between Patrick and Maria was instant and within six months they were married in a dual ceremony at Guiseley Parish Church on 29 December 1812. On this day, Patrick officiated at the wedding of his friend William Morgan, to the Fennells' daughter, also named Jane, and William married Maria and Patrick Brontë.

Maria never returned to her native Cornwall and when she sent for some of her possessions to be shipped to the north of England, the boat was wrecked in a storm. Miraculously, some of her things were rescued and returned to her. Amongst them was one of her books, written by a colleague of Patrick's at Cambridge, Henry Kirke White. This book was lost for many years but was bought and returned to the Brontë Parsonage Museum in 2016.

Patrick took his bride to his newly rented house in Clough lane, at Hightown, near Liversedge, within a mile of Hartshead Church. Here, in January 1814, their first child was born and named after her mother and was baptised by William Morgan at her father's church. A second daughter, named Elizabeth after one of her mother's sisters, was born on 8 February 1815.

By now, Patrick had made friends with the Reverend Thomas Atkinson, another friend of Morgan and Fennell, who was the minister of the church at Thornton, about six kilometres (four miles) from Bradford. The two agreed to exchange livings and Patrick was very pleased to find that his salary had doubled to around £140 per annum. The Brontë family moved to Thornton on 19 May 1815 and on the 26 August, Elizabeth Branwell was baptised at The Old Bell Chapel of St James, by John Fennell, now an ordained minister.

At the Parsonage house in Market Street, Thornton, the Brontë family lived a settled but industrious life. Patrick was busy with his parish but also writing poetry and essays and had his book, 'The Cottage in the Wood', published. They made many friends and there were teas, parties and long walks in the surrounding valleys and woodlands. However, over the next four years Maria Brontë gave birth to four more children, Charlotte, on the 21st April, 1816, Patrick Branwell, (known as Branwell), on 26 June 1817, Emily Jane on 30 July, 1818 and Anne on 17 January 1820. The house had become too small for the growing family and Patrick had his sights set on a larger and more demanding parish.

In May 1819, the perpetual curate of St Michael and All Angels Parish Church in Haworth, around thirteen kilometres (eight miles) from Thornton, died and there were discussions around who his successor should be. The trustees of the church had the right to choose their own incumbent and to refuse anyone of whom they disapproved. When the Vicar of Bradford, Henry Heap, announced to the trustees that he had chosen Patrick Brontë without consultation with them, they rejected him. The ensuing arguments and confusion led at one point to Patrick withdrawing his interest. A temporary vicar, Samuel Redhead (who again, had not been the choice of the trustees), was hounded out of town after trying on two occasions to preach to the local community. The congregation whistled, hooted and disrupted his services, even introducing a man sitting backwards on a donkey, to ride up the aisles during the sermon. After many weeks and following the congregation eventually hearing Patrick preach at Haworth, the trustees and local people warmed to him. Patrick was finally offered the position and licensed to the Perpetual Curacy in February 1820.

Saying goodbye to their friends in Thornton, the Brontë family and their servant and nursemaid, Nancy and Sarah Garrs, finally embarked for Haworth Parsonage in a number of carts on April 20 1820. Patrick, at 43 years old, was now an established and respected minister, writer and supporter of good causes. His wife had just celebrated her thirty-seventh birthday and had given birth every year for the last six years. Their eldest daughter Maria, was 6; Elizabeth, 5; Charlotte would be 4 on the following day; Branwell was 2 years and 9 months; Emily was 15 months old and Anne was a 3-month-old baby.

This move had many advantages. Although Patrick would be no better financially, he had, for his lifetime, the use of the Parsonage at

Haworth; a large and solid Georgian house standing in its own small garden above the church. The house was built, and owned, by the church trustees and contained five bedrooms, four downstairs rooms, possibly with a small back kitchen or outbuilding, and a cellar. It had its own well in the back garden and its own earth lavatory.

A full description and tour of the house will appear in a later chapter but it is important to remember that this house was above and beyond the social and financial reach of the majority of the population of Haworth and its outlying villages. Many of the 4,000 people who lived in the widespread parish shared their homes, lavatories and water supplies with many others, especially in the tight-knit communities of Haworth Township. Most families were large and the parents, often labourers, would have to manage on inadequate wages. Infant mortality stood at around one in three during the first year. After that, an average of one in five children also perished, although this was often higher, especially in times of epidemics. Overall life expectancy was only around twenty-five years. Perhaps unaware of the especially high mortality rates in his new parish, and aware that death and disease where common everywhere, Patrick Brontë very likely chose this area because of the attractive views and landscape behind their new home where lay miles of open farm and moorland; a wonderful fresh-air playground for the youngsters. The Parsonage was the highest and last house in the area and therefore separated from its neighbours. The Brontë children had room to grow and play and learn in their new house, their garden, and on the fields and moors surrounding them.

The houses in which the Brontë children were born and the churches in which their father worked, are all still standing, except the Old Bell Chapel in Thornton, which is now a romantic ruin whose walls and graveyard are kept in beautiful order by the local community. It stands opposite the current Thornton Church of St James, built in 1872, on Thornton Road. This houses the font from the Old Bell Chapel, the one in which the five youngest Brontë children were all christened. The church today offers a wonderful display of artefacts and information. The house in Hightown is in private hands but the Thornton house, at 74 Market Street, is currently a bistro and coffee house, where you can sit in the parlour where the four youngest Brontë children once lay in their cribs.

Although this book focuses on walks in and around Haworth, we felt that the importance of Thornton, its two Brontë related churches and the Brontë Birthplace were too important to miss. Therefore, we have included a walk around this special area, later in this book, and urge you to visit these sites.

Above left: Patrick Brontë in old age. Photography was in its infancy in the mid-19th century and there are no authenticated photographs of the Brontë siblings. This is, however, an actual photograph of Patrick Brontë. He is wearing the familiar white stock cloth wound around his neck to protect him from the colds and bronchitis that so affected his family. Photograph reproduced with the kind permission of the Brontë Parsonage Museum.

Above right: Portrait by J. Tonkin of Maria Branwell, future wife of Patrick Brontë. It was drawn in 1799 and is the only known picture we have of the mother of the famous Brontë siblings. Drawing reproduced with the kind permission of the Brontë Parsonage Museum.

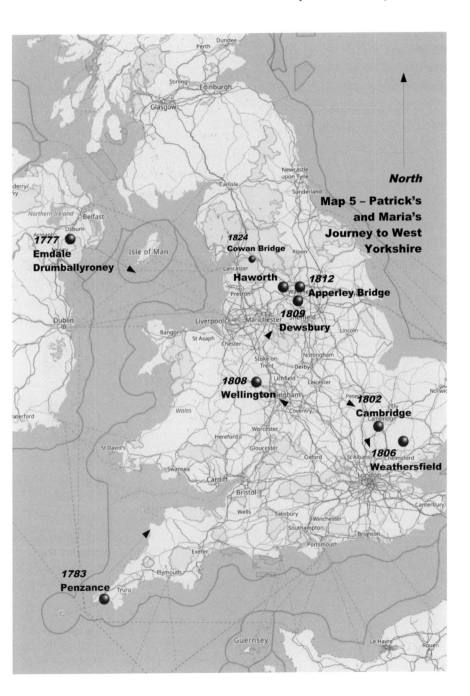

North

Map 5 – Patrick's
and Maria's
Journey to West
Yorkshire

1777
Emdale
Drumballyroney

1824
Cowan Bridge

Haworth

1812
Apperley Bridge

1809
Dewsbury

1808
Wellington

1802
Cambridge

1806
Weathersfield

1783
Penzance

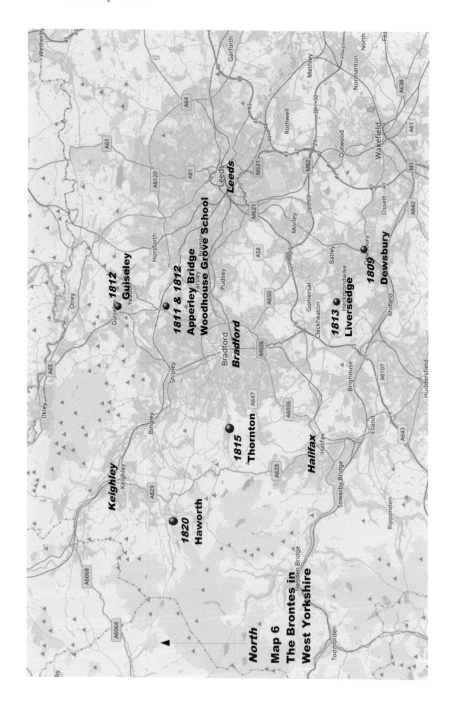

1812 Guiseley

1811 & 1812 Apperley Bridge Woodhouse Grove School

1809 Dewsbury

1813 Liversedge

1815 Thornton

Keighley

1820 Haworth

North

Map 6
The Brontes in West Yorkshire

Bronte Family Tree

Hugh Brunty *m* Alice McClory

Thomas Branwell *m* Anne Carne

Patrick - *first of ten children*
b. March 1777
d. June 1861

Elizabeth
b. Dec 1776
d. Oct 1842
(Aunt Branwell)

Maria - *fifth daughter of eleven children*
b. April 1783
d. Sept 1821

Patrick *m* Maria
Dec 1812

Maria
b. April 1814
d. May 1825

Elizabeth
b. Feb 1815
d. June 1825

Charlotte
b. April 1816
d. March 1855

m June 1854
Arthur Bell Nicholls
b. Jan 1819
d. Dec 1906

Patrick Branwell
b. June 1817
d. Sept 1848

Emily Jane
b. July 1818
d. Dec 1848

Anne
b. Jan 1820
d. May 1849

Diagram - 7

Chapter 5

The Brontës at Haworth

When the Brontë family arrived in Haworth they would have found the town larger than Thornton, the terrain much steeper, the countryside more rural and the Parsonage a rather grand detached house much bigger than their previous terraced home.

The Parsonage still stands on its elevated position overlooking the church and graveyard and the now rather quaint area of Haworth that has become a centre for tourism with its cobbled streets and teashops.

Socially, the Brontë family were in a class above the local working population but were not considered middle-class. They were relatively well catered for but had little spare money. Haworth had no schools at this time but Patrick and Maria had enough knowledge and experience to home-school their children.

All went well until Maria developed a cancer and died after a long and painful illness in September 1821. Understandably, this caused devastation and Patrick had to find someone to care for his children. His wife's sister, Elizabeth, had come to help nurse Maria and after her death she remained to look after the six children.

Elizabeth Branwell, or aunt Branwell as she was known by the children, was a spinster and had no experience of raising children. However, she did her best and taught the five girls feminine occupations and lessons and Patrick supervised Branwell. Patrick's belief in education as a means to personal and social advancement meant that he encouraged all of his children to study and gave them ample and liberal access to knowledge, including many books and journals.

The children were intelligent, if precocious, and enjoyed their studies. They had a strict Christian upbringing but had the freedom of their home and surroundings and each other to play with. They saw little of the local children and were content to rely on each other for most of their needs.

As they grew, Patrick looked for cheap but adequate schooling for his daughters to prepare them for some of the only occupations suitable for their class and circumstances, these would be as governesses or teachers. Consequently, first the two eldest, Maria and Elizabeth and then Charlotte and Emily, were sent to the Clergy Daughters' School, at Cowan Bridge in Lancashire, in 1824. Particularly set up to educate the daughters of poor clergymen, the Brontë girls were all eligible and Patrick had only to find £14 per year towards their education and board. Patrick was aware that the school was fairly new, but unaware that it had many problems and that the regime for the girls was harsh.

The Brontë sisters suffered from the cold, the poor conditions, the bad food and the lack of affection. The school day was long and delivered under a strong Calvinistic doctrine which cared more for the soul than the body. After many months of this harsh regime a number of the girls became very ill and some died. Eventually, first Maria and then Elizabeth returned home mortally ill and, tragically, they both succumbed to the combination of neglect and untreated illness which triggered, or exacerbated, tuberculosis. Patrick brought Charlotte and Emily home, where his remaining four children stayed for the next five years.

These five years saw Charlotte (now the eldest) taking the lead, but all four children worked and played together as they tried to come to terms with the loss of their mother and two sisters. Interdependent in all their work and play, they became a close unit. There was sibling rivalry but they were lively and bright children and they learned to tolerate their differences. During these years they had lessons with aunt Branwell or their father, but also a lot of free time to develop their knowledge of nature, of music and of the arts. They also had various toys and when Branwell received a new set of soldiers in June 1826, they inspired the children to develop stories based on

the adventures of these twelve 'men'. This led to a secret life of the
imagination where the children created whole islands, cities and
populations which they ruled and organised.

These childish games, at first a type of escapism, grew into a world
where each child could turn away from the reality of their actual
lives and losses. As they grew older they began to chronicle the life
and times of their make-believe places and people. This grew into
many thousands of words, recorded in tiny manuscripts containing
miniscule writings, often set out to imitate the books and journals
that they read.

As they matured, the children tended to pair off so that Charlotte
and Branwell wrote and played together and Emily and Anne did
likewise. Each pair created their own secret 'islands' and carried on
adding events and people throughout many years, possibly all of
their lives. The Glass Town Saga that had occupied them jointly,
separated to evolve into the land of Angria (Charlotte and Branwell)
and Gondal, (Emily and Anne), by the time they were all teenagers.

When Charlotte was 14 her father decided that she must have a
more refined finishing education to ready her for employment. He
sent her to Roe Head, a well-established and commendable school
near Mirfield, in Yorkshire, about twenty miles from Haworth.
Charlotte was initially homesick but soon met two pupils who
became lifelong friends, Ellen Nussey and Mary Taylor. Both girls
were from relatively wealthy families but both grew to love and
admire Charlotte's intelligence and friendship; everyone recognised
her ability to study and her talent for art and story-telling.

The inclusion of Ellen and Mary in her life, altered the Brontë
dynamics somewhat. Branwell, already isolated as the only boy and
never allowed to go away to school, may have resented the loss of
his closest sibling. Charlotte was naturally drawn towards her friends
and school took over her days and nights. She left Roe Head after
eighteen months with a Silver Medal and returned the following
term as a teacher with Emily as a pupil. Emily could not tolerate life

away from Haworth and became seriously ill; she returned home and was replaced at Roe Head by Anne.

By this time, Branwell had been receiving lessons from the Leeds portrait painter, William Robinson. The lessons cost 2 guineas each but Patrick would sacrifice any amount to encourage his children's talents. However, Branwell's efforts to set up as a portrait painter in a studio in Bradford did not succeed. He particularly wanted to be a writer but unfortunately his attempts to cajole and even bully writers and poets to publish his work were mainly met with silence, although he did manage to publish a number of poems in various local newspapers during his lifetime.

Charlotte was not a natural teacher; despite her intelligence and knowledge she had little patience with her pupils and felt that it was not her calling. In 1836, Charlotte sent some of her verse to the poet Robert Southey for his opinion. He warned her that writing 'should not be the business of a woman'. Charlotte took note but was still determined to be a writer.

By 1838, Charlotte and Anne had returned home from Roe Head School. That same year, Emily made an attempt to gain employment and earn a living. She became a teacher at Law Hill School, Southowram, near Halifax. The regime was harsh and she was very unhappy but stayed for some months. The following year Anne became a governess at Blake Hall near Mirfield, but she too found her post intolerable and left. Charlotte also took a governess post near Skipton but found the work too harsh and the children unruly, so she resigned.

Around this time a new young curate arrived in Haworth to assist Mr Brontë. The Rev. William Weightman was a charming and personable man and all the Brontës liked him. He became a close friend to Branwell and the girls found him good company as he pretended to flirt with them, and all the other eligible women in the town. Unfortunately, he succumbed to cholera (Sept 1842) and the whole family mourned his loss, especially Anne, who was possibly in love with him.

In 1840 Anne took a governess post at Thorpe Green, around twenty kilometres (twelve miles) north of York, a post she kept for five years. Branwell had found work as clerk-in-charge on the railway, at Luddenden Foot about seven kilometres (four miles) west of Halifax, in the Calder valley, regrettably he was dismissed in 1842 because of poor book-keeping and a tendency to spend his days in The Lord Nelson public house rather than at his post. Anne helped him to get a job with her as a tutor to the son of her employers, the Robinsons. Charlotte became a governess again in 1841 in Rawdon, but was both unsuited and unsuitable and soon left.

A decision was made that the sisters would try to open their own small school. To do this Charlotte persuaded her aunt and father that she and Emily should travel to the continent to learn French and German and generally gain more qualifications and experience. Aunt put up the money and the sisters travelled to Brussels and became pupils at the Pensionnat Heger, a school owned and run by Monsieur and Madame Heger. They did well there but unfortunately, Charlotte became attracted to the married M. Heger and her unrequited love made her ill for many months.

The girls returned home after aunt Branwell died in October 1842. Emily would not leave home again, but Charlotte, now besotted with M. Heger, returned to Brussels alone. She stayed for almost another year but became increasingly isolated and unhappy and eventually returned home, broken and ill.

During all of these years, the Brontës continued to write and to play out their imaginary worlds. Whereas most children grow out of this type of make-believe play and invisible people, the Brontës expanded and elaborated so that their lives had a duality in the real and the unreal. As late as June 1845, when Emily was 26 and Anne 25 years old, they had a short holiday to York, where they played out the roles of some of their imaginary Gondal characters.

By the summer of 1845, the Brontës were all back at home, all in their twenties and all unemployed. Branwell had been dismissed from his post with the Robinson family due to a liaison with his employer's wife, Lydia Robinson. Anne had already resigned because of the scandal she feared would ensue when she discovered Branwell's affair. Charlotte was still suffering from her unrequited love for M. Heger and Emily was firmly established as the main housekeeper and companion to her father.

Branwell had already begun a life of alcohol and, probably, opium abuse. His distress at having to leave Thorpe Green saw him sink into a dissolute lifestyle which horrified his family and changed him from a devoted brother and son to a man who cared nothing for himself or his family. Whilst Charlotte grieved silently and inwardly over her hopeless love for M. Heger, Branwell suffered long and loud, and turned to any palliative substance that would ease his pain. This difference separated brother and sister for the remaining years of their lives.

Towards the autumn of 1845, Charlotte discovered some poetry written by Emily and urged her to offer it for publication. Emily was horrified and deeply hurt that Charlotte had found and read her personal and secret writings and it took a long time for them to be reconciled. Anne and Charlotte both had poetry which was, they felt, good enough to be published and so after much argument and discussion, the three women put together a small collection of verse. In February 1846, Charlotte sent the manuscript to Messrs. Aylott and Jones, a London publisher. The small volume was eventually published in May 1846 at the sisters' expense but sold only two copies.

Understanding that the publishing world was very much a male dominated profession and that the sisters, Emily especially, abhorred any loss of privacy and identification, they chose to publish under pseudonyms which were androgynous but preserved their initials. They called themselves, Currer (Charlotte), Ellis (Emily) and Acton (Anne) Bell, and kept these pseudonyms throughout the rest of their publishing lives.

Sometime in 1846, and with the school idea abandoned, each sister began work on a novel with the hope that they might, one day, make enough money through writing to obviate the need to leave home and re-enter the professions they all disliked. Their manuscripts were based on their experiences and environment, all influenced by the many stories and places that they had seen or read about. Charlotte wrote, *The Professor*, Emily, *Wuthering Heights* and Anne, *Agnes Grey*. The manuscripts, wrapped up together, did the rounds of various publishers and ended up in London where *Wuthering Heights* and *Agnes Grey* were eventually accepted by publisher Thomas Newby in July 1847 and *The Professor*, whilst rejected by publishers Smith and Elder, was returned with a letter stating that they would look favourably on a work in three volumes.

Charlotte had begun the writing of *Jane Eyre* in August 1846, whilst accompanying her father in Manchester, where he spent four weeks recovering from a cataract operation. The book was almost finished and she quickly completed it and sent it to London. Six weeks later, in September 1847, it was published to wonderful reviews and became an instant bestseller. Charlotte began a long and fruitful relationship with Smith and Elder, whereas, Thomas Newby took months to publish *Wuthering Heights* and *Agnes Grey*, and the paper and production was poor and full of errors.

The success of *Jane Eyre* and the publication of Anne's next novel, *The Tenant of Wildfell Hall* in 1848, prompted the dubious Thomas Newby to suggest that Currer, Ellis and Acton Bell, were one and the same person and that person had also written *Jane Eyre*. Rather than three separate 'brothers', the suggestion was that the author was one man who was adept in the art of trickery. The authorship of the novels and the identity of the authors had set up a conundrum which many people wished to solve, not least Smith and Elder who were concerned that their bestselling author had another publisher. Much against Emily's wishes, Charlotte and Anne decided that the only way to prove that they were separate authors was to go to London and declare themselves to Smith and Elder. Emily refused to expose herself, but when her siblings arrived at the publisher's offices in London's Cornhill, Charlotte blurted out the famous line, 'We are three sisters'.

By 1848, the rumours and counter-rumours had reached Yorkshire and people began to recognise people and places in the novels. The sisters continued to deny their authorship, even when Ellen Nussey asked Charlotte outright. They all felt the need to stay anonymous so that their thoughts and feelings did not become public knowledge. Charlotte stated that she needed, 'to walk invisible'.

By 1848 Anne's controversial book *The Tenant of Wildfell Hall* was in the public domain. It told the story of the break-up, and consequences, of a failed marriage. Charlotte was writing her third book, *Shirley*. Both these books were written against the background of Branwell's increasing addictions and loss of health and self-respect. Added to this, Branwell was beginning to show all the signs of tuberculosis. By September 1848 he finally succumbed and was buried in the family vault in his father's church alongside his mother, his aunt and his two sisters.

Branwell's death was a release to him and his family, but had the profound effect that death has, in bringing an extra grief for his lost and wasted life. Within weeks, Emily too showed signs of rapid consumption. She never left the house after Branwell's funeral and refused medical treatment. Tragically, by mid-December the family were grief-stricken when Emily also lost her battle with tuberculosis and she too was buried in the family vault.

Charlotte and Anne were devastated and tormented by these deaths yet it soon became obvious that Anne's health was also of grave concern. Throughout the first months of 1849 Anne struggled against her illness and fought to stay alive. She requested a holiday in Scarborough to help her condition but she died just days after arriving by the sea. Charlotte and Ellen were beside her, and Charlotte made the decision to bury her in the town that Anne had known and loved and where she had spent summer holidays with the Robinson family. She is buried in the old St Mary's churchyard, Scarborough, overlooking the sea.

Charlotte returned home grief-stricken and profoundly lonely. Her father had only his one daughter left and he was now almost blind and in his seventy-third year. The servant, Tabby Aykroyd, was now also lame and elderly and Charlotte took on much of the housekeeping alongside the younger servant, Martha Brown. Patrick had had the help of an Irish curate, Arthur Nicholls, for some years, but he was not particularly popular with the family or, initially, with the people of Haworth. Patrick's age and failing health meant that he had to rely on him despite any personal feelings. To his credit, Mr Nicholls did his job well.

Arthur Nicholls' constant visits to the Parsonage had put him in close proximity with Charlotte but she was astounded when, in December 1852, he declared his love for her and spoke of the many months of torment he had suffered in silent heartache. When Charlotte told her father of Mr Nicholls' proposal, he was furious. Patrick had no intention of letting a humble and penniless curate marry his now famous daughter. Charlotte did however, recognise and sympathise with Mr Nicholls. She had endured long years of unrequited love and could empathise with his feelings. Nicholls was heartbroken at Patrick's resistance to any union and he resigned his post.

Charlotte's last novel, *Villette* was published in January 1853. Charlotte was by now an acknowledged author who made many visits to London and met a variety of famous people. In May 1853, the congregation of the church of St Michael and All Angels presented Mr Nicholls with a gold watch as a leaving gift for he had now arranged to work elsewhere. On the evening of 27 May, he took his leave of Mr Brontë at the Parsonage, but Charlotte was not there. Thinking he would never see her again, he left, but could not contain his grief. A short time later Charlotte found him sobbing in anguish outside the garden gate. Charlotte was moved by his devotion and her feelings towards him gradually changed. Charlotte began to write to him in secret and this continued for some months.

By January of 1854, when Mr Nicholls was staying near Haworth, he and Charlotte met and Charlotte gained permission from Patrick to continue the correspondence. Sensing failure to keep them apart, Patrick began to recognise the esteem Charlotte held for Mr Nicholls' fortitude and enduring affection and he eventually gave his permission for their union. This was not an engagement that was made in haste or in a romantic idyll, it was of the soberest kind; Charlotte recognised that she did not love Arthur Nicholls, but did have enormous affection for him which she hoped may eventually turn to love.

Marriage would, however, only take place if Mr Nicholls agreed to live at the Parsonage and help Charlotte take care of her father for the rest of his life. This was promised and they married on 29 June 1854 and honeymooned in Arthur's native Ireland. This marriage brought Charlotte a love and sense of purpose that she had not had before and she revelled in being Mrs Nicholls. Within months her affection had begun to deepen and she was extremely attentive to her husband's feelings and welfare.

All was well until Charlotte developed a cold in January and felt weak and sickly. It was the beginnings of pregnancy – and the start of a fatal return of tuberculosis. For weeks Charlotte was ill and confined to bed before dying, aged 39, on 31 March 1855, only nine months after her wedding day. Mr Nicholls was heartbroken but continued to look after Mr Brontë as promised. The last and oldest member of the Brontë family, Patrick, died in June 1861 in his eighty-fifth year and the Rev. Nicholls returned to Ireland.

Diagram 8 – First Publications of Books by the Bronte Sisters

Currer Bell = Charlotte Bronte, Ellis Bell = Emily Bronte, Acton Bell = Anne Bronte

1846	May	***'Poems by Currer, Ellis and Acton Bell'*** Published by Aylott and Jones, Paternoster Row, London.
1847	Oct	***'Jane Eyre'*** by Currer Bell Published by Smith, Elder and Company, Cornhill, London.
1847	Dec	***'Wuthering Heights and Agnes Grey'*** by Ellis and Acton Bell in three volumes. Published by Thomas Cautley Newby, Mortimer Street, Cavendish Square, London. The novels were not published separately until after Emily and Anne's deaths, (*Wuthering Heights:* Emily, *Agnes Grey:* Anne).
1848	June	***'The Tenant of Wildfell Hall'*** by Acton Bell Published by Thomas Cautley Newby, Mortimer Street, Cavendish Square, London.
1849	Oct	***'Shirley. A Tale'*** by Currer Bell Published by Smith, Elder and Company, Cornhill, London.
1853	Jan	***'Villette'*** by Currer Bell Published by Smith, Elder and Company, Cornhill, London.
1857	June	***'The Professor'*** by Currer Bell 'The Professor' was published posthumously by Smith, Elder and Company, Cornhill, London.

Above: Haworth Parsonage showing the original house, built in 1778. This photograph was taken in the 1860's and shows various Haworth residents in and around the graveyard. The lady nearest to the Parsonage is not one of the Brontë girls, they had all died by the time this photograph was taken. However, it does show how the house looked around the time of Patrick Brontë's death in 1861. Photograph reproduced with the kind permission of the Brontë Parsonage Museum.

Below: Haworth Parsonage showing the part of the building that existed from 1778 before the additional wing of the 1880's added by the next incumbent, the Rev John Wade, Patrick Brontë's successor.

Above: Autumn in Haworth church graveyard with the Parsonage partially hidden behind the trees.

Left: St Michael and All Angels' church, viewed from the east and showing the line of the original roof before the rebuilding in the 1880's.

Above: The overcrowded graveyard of Haworth church highlighting the unhealthy habit of table and flat top gravestones.

Below: The full frontage of Haworth parsonage today showing part of the well-kept garden.

Chapter 6

A guided tour of The Brontë Parsonage Museum

Walk 1

When you come to Haworth, walk up the steep Main Street and you will come to a small square surrounded by shops and various public houses, with the church of St Michael and All Angels on your left-hand side above a flight of stone steps. Moving across the square you reach the narrow Church Street on your left, beside the King's Arms public house. You will soon come to the old over-crowded graveyard and see the Parsonage above it and the Old School Rooms on your right. Walk towards the Parsonage and at the top of the lane on your left, enter the 1960s' extension where there are offices, a reception area and the Parsonage book shop. After purchasing your ticket at the reception desk walk around to the front of the building and enter the garden by the side gate.

If you stand in the beautifully laid out garden and look towards the house you will note the symmetry of the original Georgian dwelling built in 1778/9. The elegant doorway is flanked by two windows and above are three bedroom windows. The extension to your right-hand side was built in the 1880s, when the next incumbent following Patrick Brontë, the Rev. Wade, extended that side of the house.

The Parsonage faces east towards the church tower. At the time of the Brontës' arrival there were no schoolrooms across the street but a barn stood where part of the car park is now laid out. The house had gardens at the front, sides and back and was surrounded by a wall.

If you stand with the house behind you, note a plaque in the east garden wall showing where there was originally a walkway from the garden to the church door. When the Brontës lived here there were no trees to shelter the house and grounds from the weather, and the graveyard was rapidly filling from the hundreds of burials that were typical of a town where there was poverty and disease.

You will enter the house into a pleasant hallway from which rises the staircase. Immediately to your left is the parlour. This served as the dining room, sitting room and schoolroom for the Brontës. As now, all the ground floor was stone-flagged and mainly peat was burned in the fireplaces in an attempt to keep the rooms warm. The risk of fire caused Patrick Brontë to forbid the use of draperies and at night the wooden shutters would help to keep out the cold wind and rains.

The Brontës were not wealthy and lived only on their father's stipend for most of their lives. Furniture and furnishings would have been basic and simple, though well made. In this room you will see the original table used by the family and returned to the Parsonage only in 2016. It is the table on which the sisters wrote their novels and poetry and on which, at one time, their brother also studied and wrote. As they grew older Patrick bought them each a writing desk and these are displayed around the museum. This room houses some of the books owned by the family and also contains an old settle which is thought to be original to the family. Legend states that Emily may have died on this piece of furniture. The walls are now papered with a pattern taken from an original drawing designed by Charlotte. Two hundred years ago the walls were only painted, in a light, dove-grey colour. At the time of writing, this room and others in the house contain costumes from the recent film on the Brontës entitled '*To Walk Invisible*' (2016).

The parlour contains many possessions that were owned and used by the Brontë family and it is worth a long look at the different articles on display. Above the fireplace is the portrait of Charlotte by

George Richmond, drawn in chalks in 1850. When Charlotte first saw it she became distressed because she thought it reminded her of her sisters who had died the previous year. Whilst standing here, imagine the room in candlelight or firelight with the shutters closed and the wind blowing and the Brontë sisters writing furiously on the table in front of you, or wandering round it and quoting scenes from their new novels.

If you stand in the doorway of the parlour and look along the line of the wall towards the front door, you will note that this door looks to be offset rather than central. This is because as Charlotte grew wealthier in her last few years, she made various alterations to the house. This included enlarging the parlour to make it more accommodating to guests. These changes involved remodelling the hallway and adding the arch. The removal and rebuilding of the wall was also carried through to the upstairs and reduced the size of the small bedroom and enlarged the front bedroom on your right at the top of the stairs.

Across the hallway from the parlour was Patrick Brontë's study. This room contains various artefacts belonging to him and also Emily's piano and some of the pictures, notably biblical scenes by John Martin, that were there when the Brontës occupied the house. Emily was a talented musician and Patrick was always willing to spend his money on encouraging his children's abilities. The mahogany piano was probably made in London but purchased locally. Known as a Cottage piano it has only five octaves with the strings disguised behind a pleated silk screen. The piano is still playable but very delicate and is regularly maintained by a fund set up by a member of the Brontë Society.

The study is the room that Patrick Brontë used for over forty years to plan his work and write his many sermons, letters and tracts. Over time he became expert at *extempore* sermons where he spoke directly from memory and experience. Patrick will have entertained many visiting parishioners and clergy in this room and it was, at times, his safe and peaceful sanctuary from the noise and events of his busy life and household. The view of his church dominated this room and his life and one can well imagine him seated before the fire, or busy at his writing desk where a glance through the window reassured him of his faith and purpose.

Two arched recesses along the wall on either side of the doorway were probably filled with his many books which he enthusiastically encouraged his children to read. Today this room, like some of the others, has been wallpapered with a design created by Charlotte when she began to upgrade her home and make it more comfortable and in keeping with Victorian middle classes. For most of their lives the Parsonage may have been sparsely furnished but it was always kept scrupulously clean.

During the time the Brontës lived here there were Georgian sash windows and no curtains. The windows have been replaced over the years and the current ones are designed for security and to stop natural light fading the collection. This is why some of the rooms often feel shut in and a little gloomy, with blinds and tinted glass. There is a sound reason for this as it will help to reduce the light that fades and damages articles and furnishings, so maintaining the collection for future generations. Similarly, many artefacts are held under special glass with temperature and light control. Whilst it would be lovely to handle and examine these precious relics it would greatly accelerate their deterioration.

Millions of people have visited Haworth Parsonage since it was donated to the Brontë Society in 1928 by Sir James Roberts and that has brought its own problems. Like all museums the house is loved and visited but each person adds to the wear and tear of the structure and its contents. The Brontë Society are vigilant in their efforts to preserve and maintain the Parsonage and its exhibits. The collection of Brontë memorabilia is the largest in the world and the staff circulate objects and introduce new ones from storage, so that it can all be displayed over time in the limited space.

Diagonally opposite Patrick's study is a room known as 'Mr Nicholl's study'. Formally the peat room it was where storage of peat, goods, animals, food etc. was apparently kept until Charlotte redecorated and furnished it into her husband's study. Although this room has always been here, like the bedrooms, it will have been used for many functions over the years. Whereas the use of the parlour or sitting room, the kitchen and Patrick's study probably remained constant, the other rooms will have been utilised for whatever function was needed at the time. Visitors would have stayed at the Parsonage and various events, such as illness and death for example, would have meant a change in usage of various rooms over the years. It is likely that all the Brontës slept in all of the bedrooms at different times and for different reasons and this 'spare' room behind the parlour could have had many functions as circumstances altered.

Later in your tour we will recommend that you step out into the back garden of the house and observe the different architecture and array of blocked up windows and doors and the chimney flues. Various ideas have been put forward over the years as to which rooms had fireplaces, windows and exit doors and this is still not completely clear as so much has changed over time.

As you leave Mr Nicholl's study you will see on your left a door which leads down into the cellar via a short, turning, stone staircase, which has a small window letting in light. The original cellar was a small vaulted room under the kitchen and still exists. During the building of the new north wing of the house in the 1880s, a doorway was created from the small cellar to a much larger one with another leading off it where coal and fuel were stored. These newer rooms are used today for talks and education programmes as a temporary measure until more space is acquired. They are only open to the public on these occasions.

Passing the staircase, you may now enter the small kitchen, perhaps the most altered of the downstairs rooms. The 1880s wing started from this room and the doorway you see beside the Victorian range leads to what is now the Parsonage library. The library is available for scholars, by request, for academic study. The curator also holds special events where enthusiasts can see, handle and learn about special items from the collection. It houses every book written on the Brontës and much more besides.

As you stand in the kitchen entrance you will note another door to your left. This leads through to the 1960s' extension built on to the back of the Parsonage, originally for the curator and to make extra space for the growing collection and staff. Between these two doors would have been a window. There was also a back kitchen or scullery where the laundry and heavy work was done and this was probably added in the Brontës' time. From the kitchen a doorway, probably the one on your left, led to the yard, garden and outer kitchen. There was also, possibly, another door from the kitchen leading from the north side of the house to the outside lane (Church Street).

The kitchen was small and cramped but had to serve the needs of many people. The Brontës kept various servants and housemaids over the years as befitted their status but it cannot have been an easy room to work in and provide meals, with no modern conveniences. The smells, sounds and general clamour of the kitchens will have infiltrated the house from early morning until late at night. When the Brontës arrived in 1820 this kitchen served ten people; Mr and Mrs Brontë, their six children all under 7 years, a housemaid and a nursemaid. This was not a large house for so many but it was enormous compared with the living conditions of most of the inhabitants of Haworth at that time.

It is interesting to imagine the amount of washing and drying that ten people, three of them under 3, would generate in a week and it is by doing this imaginary 'time travel' that we can more thoroughly appreciate the lives of people 200 years ago. Even today, how many of us could create even one meal for ten people on an open fire with a side oven? How much hard labour would be involved in soaking, washing, wringing and drying bedding and clothing with only a wash tub, a dolly stick and a bar of soap? Where would it be dried on wet and foggy days?

It is important to think about the conditions and the minimal appliances the people had to work with. Patrick Brontë had only a modest income and he had a great deal of expense. Food and shelter would have to be the priority and yet he managed to educate and school all of his children in many different areas of art, literature and science. The Brontë children spent many hours in this room, the warmest in the house, helping with chores and listening to servant gossip!

Moving to the staircase one can climb the stone steps and see a recess at the first turn and a large window. The recess was probably always there but it became a doorway for the new wing and led to bedrooms and bathrooms in the 1880s. It now houses a grandfather clock which belonged to the family and was attended to by Patrick each night on his way to bed. The window was formerly longer and would have allowed views across the back garden and across to the moors and was a good source of light.

As you ascend the stairs you will see a copy of the 'Pillar Portrait' painted by Branwell of his sisters. Branwell painted himself out of this portrait but we do not know why. The original portrait has, over time, deteriorated but, ironically, this is now causing the self-portrait that Branwell tried to obliterate to slowly re-emerge through the canvas. It can be viewed at its permanent home in The National Portrait Gallery in London.

It is important to remember that the use of rooms change over time. As the family grew and then shrank and as different servants and guests came to stay, rooms would be reallocated. The Brontë Society has labelled the rooms according to how they were most commonly used in the last years of the Brontë family's occupation.

The first room to the right at the top of the stairs was possibly the servants' room. This would allow for the free movement of the various servants to access the stairs early in the morning without disturbing the household. It corresponds to Mr Nicholl's study below and probably had a fireplace and a window. It was once thought that it may have been served by an external staircase but no real evidence has been found. The window, as below, looks out on to the graveyard.

The next room, at the front of the house, is labelled as Charlotte's room. It was enlarged for Charlotte at the same time as the downstairs parlour. It was formerly Patrick and Maria Brontë's bedroom and later the room where aunt Branwell settled when she came to look after her nephew and nieces. Eventually this room became Charlotte's and she later shared it with her husband in the nine months before her death. The staff regularly change the exhibits in here and there are lots of written details to help you identify the artefacts. Remember that the staff and volunteers who work here are always around the rooms to help and advise and to answer any questions you may wish to ask. Again we see a room that changed over time from a cosy bedroom to a sickroom and a death chamber to a bed-sitting room for aunt Branwell and a schoolroom, where she instructed her nieces and taught them to sew. After her death the sisters possibly had their own bedrooms for the first time in their lives, or they may have continued to share as they always had done. This room has served the inhabitants of the house for over 240 years and has witnessed all the scenes and events of many births, lives and deaths before, during and after the Brontës' time here.

Returning to the landing you can now see on your right between the two front bedrooms the small middle room labelled as the childrens' study. Look again at the walls between this room and the adjacent bedroom to your right and note how the wall has been moved, as below, to create bigger rooms. This has reduced the size of this middle room and set the window off to one side. It would have previously accommodated a single bed and was probably the nursery or a child's bedroom. It could be that the children used it as a study at times or it could have been a servant's room. Perhaps after her marriage Charlotte used it as a dressing room? We do not know but we can speculate and we can imagine the constant movement around the various rooms and their changes of use. There are various drawings on the walls of this room but it is suspect as to when these occurred. It is nice to think they may have been done by the Brontë children, but it seems unlikely. In one of her diary papers Emily draws a picture seemingly of this room with a bed under the window and a chest of drawers to the left. It is a pleasant room with plenty of light yet it had no fireplace and, being over the entrance hall, had no heat from below, so would have been very cold in the winter months.

On leaving this small room turn to your right and enter the remaining front bedroom which became Patrick's bedroom in his later years. As Branwell's health deteriorated and his behaviour became more unpredictable, including causing a fire in his own room, his father brought him into this room to sleep with him for his own protection. Branwell probably died in this room in 1848 and his father in 1861. There is a replica bed based on a drawing by Branwell which is a typical bed of the time. The chest of drawers was owned by the family as was most of the other furniture in the room. Like the study below it, it looks out over the church and graveyard and, as all the rooms in the house, it would have echoed to the church bells and clock, day and night.

The last bedroom from the landing is labelled as Branwell's room and probably was at one time. He may also have used it as his art studio for a while. This room has recently been furnished with many of the props from the film *To Walk Invisible* (2016) and offers a wonderful insight into how Branwell's room might have looked and portrays his chaotic lifestyle of later years. The room would have had a window overlooking the back of the house with a wonderful view across the moorland. This may have been partly obliterated when Patrick had the back kitchen built. It is difficult to know the exact dimensions of the outbuildings.

The upstairs of the 1880s' wing leads from this room to the north side of the house. None of the rest of the museum existed in the time of the Brontës, but was all added afterwards. The Reverend Wade, quite rightly, wanted more space and luxury for his household and was not willing to have his home turned into a shrine to the previous famous family. He made alterations with no sensitivity to the Parsonage as a place of homage and repelled visitors who wanted admittance.

You now enter what were his new bedrooms and bathrooms and is currently an open plan area of the museum housing many precious Brontë relics and an exhibition of their life story. A particular feature of the room is the 'Apostles Cupboard', a rare piece of furniture which was formerly owned by the Eyre family of North Lees, Hathersage, in Derbyshire. The cupboard has a long history and was seen by Charlotte when she visited Hathersage with her friend Ellen Nussey and is described by Charlotte in *Jane Eyre*. It was during her stay in Derbyshire that Charlotte consciously, or unconsciously, collected many names, situations, people and settings for her book. This priceless piece of furniture was offered to the Brontë Society in 1935 and purchased for £25! It is well worth spending time in this room following the Brontë story and seeing all of the collection housed here; each piece poignantly linked to the family's extraordinary lives and tragic deaths.

On leaving this room via the staircase one finds on the left a room that houses the Bonnell Collection and is often used for exhibitions. Many people have donated items to the museum over the years. One of the most notable was Henry Houston Bonnell of Philadelphia, USA. During his lifetime this affluent businessman became well known as a collector of fine arts. A regular buyer at Southerbys,

Mr Bonnell bought a huge collection of Brontëana from all over the world. Under the terms of his will his widow sent to the Parsonage a total of 336 items which make up some of the museums greatest treasures and this generosity helped to encourage others to donate their precious items. Mr Bonnell's remaining Brontë possessions were donated to the Pierpont Morgan Library in New York and the Brontë Society sometimes exhibits items from their collection in a complementary and mutual exchange.

It must be noted that after Patrick Brontë's death in 1861 and Mr Nicholl's decision to move back to Ireland, almost all of the contents not previously given away or desired by Mr Nicholls, were auctioned. The sale took place over two days in October 1861 and contained 485 lots. Many of these items have been bought over the years and donated back to the Parsonage. The auction catalogue is a hugely informative record of what was in the house and thousands of individual items have been returned over many years and are still coming up for auction or being given to the Society. It is this vast collection that informs scholars and interested parties about the lives of this remarkable family and the Brontë Society is committed to its care and preservation.

Beside the Bonnell room is a small area which often houses a current exhibition and this changes regularly according to themes and events. Between 2016 and 2020 the bicentenaries of each of the four youngest Brontë siblings occurs and the Society has organised major and minor events, conferences, exhibitions, lectures and outings to celebrate the 200th anniversary of each of their births.

As you move now into an open area you can see the doors on your left leading out into a small garden. You are now in the 1960s extension but if you pass through the doors to the outside you will be able to see the west wall of the house and some of the garden. Most of the back wall is visible and shows a remarkable variety of lintels and doorways and window frames no longer in use. This gives a small insight into how the house was originally laid out.

Behind you is the extension which took over much of the previous garden which surrounded the property. Towards a corner of the west garden wall would have been the privy and in the flowered space the original well.

There is a statue in this garden of the three sisters which was sculpted by Jocelyn Horner in 1951 and presented to the Brontë Society. Sit out here on the wooden bench and try to imagine it all 200 years ago. Listen to the birds and the church bells, smell the flowers and take yourself back in time.

Returning indoors note the photographs and pictures on display and then descend the short flight of steps down into the Parsonage bookshop. This shop helps to support the enormous costs of running and maintaining the museum and is a treasure trove of books and items for the discerning shopper.

When you leave the building do not return immediately to your car or to the town but turn to your left and observe a meadow and a field owned and used by the Brontë Society. It is a haven of wildlife and wildflowers and you are welcome to stroll around it. You will have a view of Penistone Hill and the moors.

Returning down Church Street remember to observe the north wall of the Parsonage on your right, now the Wade wing, and note where there have been windows and doors in the past. Opposite this wall is a small green area owned by the Brontë Society and was the original site of the old barn which stood during the Brontës' time and was used by the sexton. As you walk down the lane towards the church note the buildings on your left. This is the old school room built in Patrick's time with subscriptions he helped to raise. The two west gables were added separately at a later date, but still in the nineteenth century. His daughters and son all taught at the Sunday school here at various times. It houses some lovely photographs of Haworth over the years and is run by a local group named Brontë Spirit. The buildings are the property of the church. The end house was built in the Brontës' time by the sexton, John Brown, in 1838.

Mr Nicholls lodged here when he was Patrick's curate. On your right is the church and the graveyard. This lovely cobbled lane leads back down beside The King's Arms into the small square at the top of Main Street.

Fact File – Walk 1: Tour of the Brontë Parsonage Museum.

Start/Finish – Grid ref: SE 028 373

OS Maps: OL21 (1:25,000), Landranger 104 (1:50,000)

Church Street, Haworth, behind St Michael and All Angels Church.

Purchase of ticket required to enter the museum. Allow 2-3 hours.

General Information – bookshop, but no current toilet or cafe facilities inside museum, (plenty of facilities close by in town), plus pay and display car parks immediately to north of Church Street, access off Main Street, (West Street Car Park), and North Street, (Changegate Car Park).

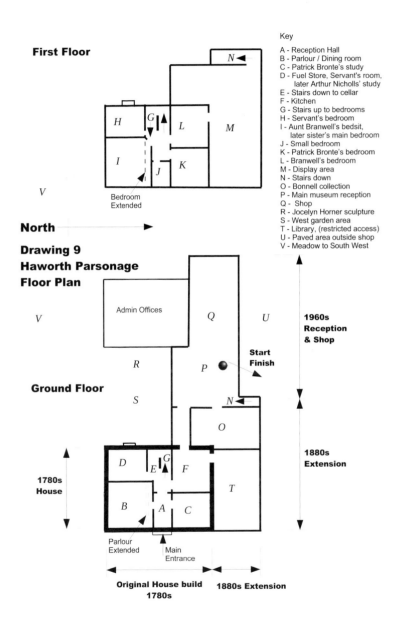

First Floor

Key

A - Reception Hall
B - Parlour / Dining room
C - Patrick Bronte's study
D - Fuel Store, Servant's room,
   later Arthur Nicholls' study
E - Stairs down to cellar
F - Kitchen
G - Stairs up to bedrooms
H - Servant's bedroom
I - Aunt Branwell's bedsit,
   later sister's main bedroom
J - Small bedroom
K - Patrick Bronte's bedroom
L - Branwell's bedroom
M - Display area
N - Stairs down
O - Bonnell collection
P - Main museum reception
Q - Shop
R - Jocelyn Horner sculpture
S - West garden area
T - Library, (restricted access)
U - Paved area outside shop
V - Meadow to South West

Bedroom
Extended

North

**Drawing 9
Haworth Parsonage
Floor Plan**

Admin Offices

**1960s
Reception
& Shop**

Start
Finish

Ground Floor

**1880s
Extension**

**1780s
House**

Parlour
Extended

Main
Entrance

**Original House build
1780s**

1880s Extension

Above: Church Street leading to Haworth Parsonage and showing the 1830's National Sunday School on the right hand side. This building was erected through the efforts of Patrick Brontë with public subscriptions and a grant.

Below: Looking down Church Street with the Sunday school gable extensions to the left and the Parsonage wall to the right.

Right: The garden gate on Church Street leading in to the front entrance of the Parsonage

Below: Picture of the Parsonage garden taken from the east garden wall, showing the Parsonage.

Above: Inside the Parsonage to the left by the front door is the Parlour. Here one can view the original table, on which the sisters wrote their famous novels. When visiting, note George Richmond's portrait of Charlotte hung over the fireplace and the sofa on which Emily probably died. Photograph reproduced with the kind permission of the Brontë Parsonage Museum.

Below: Patrick Brontë's study showing Emily's cottage piano and various articles and pictures belonging to the Brontë family, including Patrick's top hat and spectacles. Photograph reproduced with the kind permission of the Brontë Parsonage Museum.

A view from the top of the staircase looking down on to the Barraclough, longcase, grandfather clock. A copy of the famous Pillar Portrait painted by Branwell of his three sisters, adorns the wall as you walk up the steps on to the landing. The original is in the National Portrait Gallery. Photograph reproduced with the kind permission of the Brontë Parsonage Museum.

A mock-up of Branwell's bedroom to demonstrate how it may have looked during his adulthood. The props are from the Brontë film, 'To Walk Invisible' 2016. Branwell used this room as both bedroom and art room at times before a careless fire forced him to share his father's bedroom for everyone's safety. Photograph reproduced with the kind permission of the Brontë Parsonage Museum.

A view of the back of the original house, which, with a bit of investigation, will indicate the many alterations made over the centuries. There are bricked up doors and windows and redundant chimneys. The 1960's extension obliterates much of the rest of the back of the house.

The view of the church today, as seen from the Parsonage; much changed since the time of the Brontës.

Chapter 7

A guided walk around Haworth church

Walk 2

Having left the Parsonage and walked down Church Street you will see on your right the side entrance to the church of St Michael and All Angels. Visitors are welcome throughout the day to come inside and view this beautiful building with its many Brontë connections. Like most churches this is an active area where people have worshipped for centuries. It is constantly in use and is an important part of the town and its history.

Over the years it too has been altered, rebuilt and refurbished in an ongoing cycle. During the past few years it has had another major renovation both of its roof and tower and the reordering of the western end of the building to provide more amenities. The cost of this enormous project was met as the result of a huge effort to raise funds locally and also to attract grants of nearly three quarters of a million pounds. The church is now sound and waterproof for another century but still needs rewiring, restoration cleaning and redecorating. Keeping it alive and serviceable never stops and like all buildings, it has to adapt and revise its purpose according to the times and the people it provides for.

A church has stood on this site for at least 700 years and possibly much longer. The only original part of the fifteenth-century building, known to the Brontë family and still standing, is the base of the church tower which must be viewed from the outside where you can see the tiny doorway which opens on to a spiral, stone staircase which ascends to the roof of the tower. When you have viewed the church from the inside, walk around the outside of the building and note the line of the roof against the tower and see where the Brontë church roof was originally aligned. Some photographs exist of the church at the time of the Brontës and we have included one amongst the photographs at the end of this chapter.

The church was virtually rebuilt in the late 1870s and early 1880s but this was necessary because of the unhealthy and dangerous state of both church and graveyard and the effect on its congregation. The church of the Brontë's time had stood since 1655 and was enlarged and altered during the incumbency of the famous Reverend Grimshaw a hundred years later. This was the church which the Brontë family knew and it was a damp, dark and dismal building during Patrick's incumbency. Many of the windows were partly covered because of the raised organ loft and the public gallery that ran around three sides. A three-decker pulpit dominated the south wall and the box pews and lack of safe lighting also restricted light and fresh air. Patrick Brontë did a great deal to try and improve the sanitation of the town and of the church and graveyard and his efforts helped to bring fresh water and drainage to the area but, unfortunately, too late for his own family.

As you walk into the church today you see a clean and airy building which has a long history and a number of treasures. It is a much larger church than the previous one although covering some of same ground and probably using some of the stone of the original. To your right against the west wall is the newly installed amenities area containing café facilities and toilets and is currently developing for the sale of goods and for meetings. It is the next exciting stage in its development as a social arena.

Near the entrance you will see the two memorials commemorating the men of Haworth and surrounding villages who died in the two world wars. As you walk down this first aisle notice the picture windows and the memorial to William Weightman; Mr Brontë's lively and much loved curate who tragically died from cholera in 1842 at the age of 28. He was a friend to Branwell and the Brontë sisters and once, on discovering that the girls had never received a Valentine card, he walked all the way to Halifax to post them one each. They referred to him affectionately as Miss Celia Amelia, and they all grieved for him. Patrick described him as being 'like a son' when he preached his memorial service. It is thought that Anne may have especially held William Weightman in high esteem and in her book *Agnes Grey* the heroine marries her kind and caring curate. Anne wrote some poetry which has been interpreted as showing her grief over the death of Weightman. These two verses express the feelings of a person in deep mourning and are from Anne's poem entitled, 'A Reminiscence'

Yes, though art gone and never more
Thy sunny smile shall gladden me;
But I may pass the old church door,
And pace the floor that covers thee

May stand upon the cold, damp stone,
And think that frozen, lies below
The lightest heart that I have known,
The kindest I shall ever know.

Anne Brontë. 1844

It is both easy and presumptuous to assume that a poem or a book reflects actual events and feelings and it is impossible to know now how Anne felt or whether this poem refers to her mother and sisters, or no one special at all. It is, however, a poignant few lines which many people can identify with.

Observing the lovely stained-glass windows note the 'Doctor's Window' placed here in 1939 in memory of Dr Joseph Connell Wilson and his family. He was a much loved local physician in the area at the turn of the twentieth century.

In the north-east corner, standing before the organ, you will see the font which is made of alabaster supported on marble columns. Alabaster is a soft mineral rock of gypsum or calcite, it is normally white or translucent and is suitable for carving. This font was the gift of Mrs George Merrall, who was married to a local mill owner. The original stone font, donated by the Rev. Grimshaw and used by Patrick Brontë was missing for many years, possibly taken when the church was rebuilt in the 1880s. It was returned in 1929 and now stands in the graveyard to the south of the church.

The organ you are now looking at was built in to this space in 1883 by a Leeds firm of organ-builders, J. J. Binns of Bramley. The organ was hand-pumped at that time but it was renovated in 1975 and further in 1991 when more stops were added and the console was moved to its current position. In the Brontës' time there was no organ initially and music was provided by local musicians. Patrick raised funds to have an organ installed during his ministry. It was a complicated instrument but Branwell learnt to play it.

Moving towards the altar, the Choir Stalls are made of solid oak which are each beautifully and individually decorated. The Rector's stall shows carved animals from scenes in the Book of Revelations.

Alabaster features again as you move into the Chancel. The alabaster chancel screen and pulpit were donated by George Firth and contain scenes from the Gospel of St. Luke. Behind the altar is a reredos of Derbyshire alabaster depicting Leonardo Da Vinci's, 'The Last Supper'. This was presented to the new church by Mrs Wade, the wife of the Rev. John Wade who took up the incumbency after Patrick Brontë, from 1861 to 1898.

The five light, 'Te Deum' east window, situated behind the altar and above the reredos, shows biblical scenes in beautiful stained glass.

To the right of the altar is the Bronte Memorial Chapel which was dedicated to the family in 1964 by the Bishop of Bradford and was funded by Sir Tresham Lever, a long-time supporter of the Brontë Society. This beautiful chapel contains articles from the Grimshaw and Brontë period including the old communion table and, on the south wall, the original Brontë memorial stone.

Beneath the floor of the altar and the Brontë chapel lies the crypt containing the remains of the Brontë family and a brass plate on the floor marks the spot. All the Brontë family were buried here except for Anne who died in Scarborough and, as mentioned earlier, is buried there in the graveyard of St Mary's church high up on the south cliff below the castle walls. The Brontë crypt was sealed many years ago and there is no longer access. The Brontë memorial tablet gives the dates of birth and death for the whole family who lie beneath. All of the woodwork in the Brontë chapel was lovingly carved by local craftsmen and it is a still, calm place for silent prayer and reflection.

Moving down the aisle against the south wall you will notice a glass-covered cabinet containing various documents recording important dates in the lives and deaths of the Brontë family. Once again there are various beautiful stained-glass windows including one known as the 'Brontë' or 'American Window', donated by an American named Thomas Hockley who was a particular admirer of Charlotte Brontë and her writing. It contains the text, 'Anything you did for one of my brothers here, however humble, you did for me.' The inscription reads 'To the Glory of God in pleasant memory of Charlotte Brontë by an American citizen'.

Near this window hangs a wooden board which names most of the Incumbents of the church over the last 500 years, including Patrick Brontë who was its longest serving minister in the forty-one years from 1820 to 1861. Missing from this board is a man whose name is not commemorated. He was the Rev. Edmund Robinson 1688–89, who had a profitable side line as a 'coiner'; someone who forged money often by 'clipping' bits off gold and silver coins. In 1691 he was eventually sentenced to hang after passing many thousands of pounds worth of fake coins.

The west window shows the twelve apostles and was donated by the Taylor family. Throughout the church you will also see many wall paintings. One of the clearest is on the wall of the vestry and depicts Jesus on a donkey riding into Jerusalem on Palm Sunday.

Do not limit yourself to the items we have identified. The church is beautiful, warm and welcoming and you will find your own interesting artefacts and enjoy the calm. There is often some gentle music playing which adds to the atmosphere.

Again one can imagine the church over the centuries when it had boxed pews, rush lights and the three-decker pulpit from which both the evangelical Reverends Grimshaw and Brontë preached to the people of Haworth. The top part of this pulpit still exists and can be found in St Gabriel's Chapel of Ease on the main street in the neighbouring village of Stanbury, two kilometres north-west of Haworth.

There is a door in the south wall which will take you back outside into the graveyard but if it is locked, leave by the main entrance. We strongly recommend that you now walk around the outside of the church and note the architecture and setting and examine the old original lower church tower. This is pitted with small holes from Patrick Brontë discharging the pistol he kept by his bedside at night for protection. The covered entrance in the south wall was probably the original doorway into the church before it was enlarged.

The church has four clocks on the sides of the tower thus facing each compass direction. These were installed after the raising of the tower by 9ft, (3 metres) in 1870 to accommodate them. Originally, there was one clock on the east side of the tower overlooking Main Street. The current church bells were raised by subscription in 1845, initiated and organised by Patrick Brontë, and they replaced those from the 1700s. The 1845 bells were overhauled in 1933 and rehung.

As you wander around the inside and outside of the building you may be able to work out exactly where its predecessors stood and what has been altered. It is fascinating to work out the changes and to imagine it back in time. The photographs and drawings in this chapter should help you with this. A church has existed here during enormous social changes and served the community of Haworth for centuries past. Hopefully it will do so for many more to come.

Fact File – Walk 2: Tour of Haworth Church.

Start/Finish – Grid ref: SE 030 372

OS Maps: OL21 (1:25,000), Landranger 104 (1:50,000)

Entrance off Church Street, west of Main Street, Haworth.

Please make a donation. Allow 1-1.5 hours.

General Information – toilets and refreshments are available during some church events. Plenty of facilities close by in the town centre.

Pay and display car parks, only a short walk to north of the church.

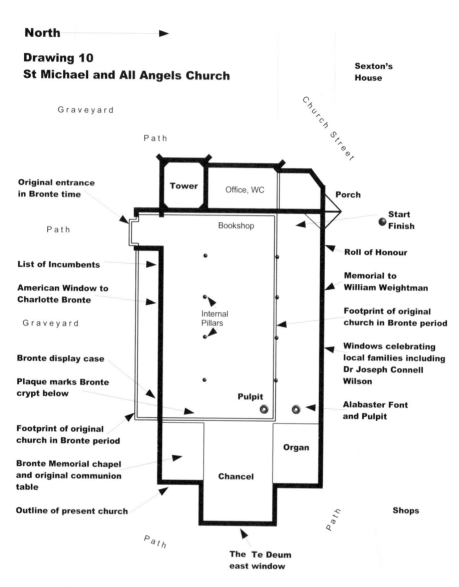

North ──────────▶

**Drawing 10
St Michael and All Angels Church**

Sexton's
House

Graveyard

Church Street

Path

Tower

Office, WC

Porch

**Original entrance
in Bronte time**

Start
Finish

Path

Bookshop

Roll of Honour

List of Incumbents

**Memorial to
William Weightman**

**American Window to
Charlotte Bronte**

**Footprint of original
church in Bronte period**

Graveyard

Internal
Pillars

**Windows celebrating
local families including
Dr Joseph Connell
Wilson**

Bronte display case

**Plaque marks Bronte
crypt below**

Pulpit

**Alabaster Font
and Pulpit**

**Footprint of original
church in Bronte period**

**Bronte Memorial chapel
and original communion
table**

Organ

Chancel

Outline of present church

Path

Shops

Path

**The Te Deum
east window**

**The Black
Bull Inn**

Steps down to Main Street

Above: A view of Haworth Church in the Brontës' time, viewed from the south-west. All of this original tower was incorporated in the 1880s 'new' church, though increased in height to accommodate the clock faces, as pictured below.

Below: A view of Haworth Church as it looks today, taken from the south-west.

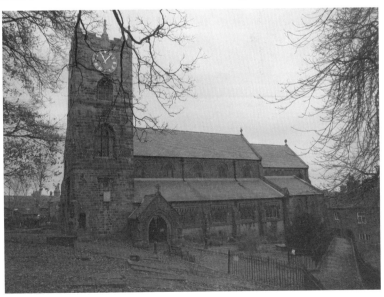

Above: Looking west up Church Street at the church entrance.

Left: The wall mounted marble mural to the dead of the First World War.

Above: The Roll of Honour commemorating the soldiers from Haworth who fought in the two World Wars.

Right: The monument erected by the local people, in memory of the popular curate, William Weightman, who died of cholera in 1842 aged 28 years.

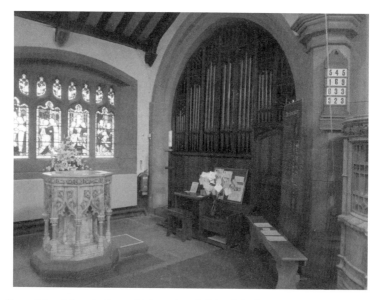

Above: The alabaster font which replaced the original stone one used for many years and now in the graveyard. The current organ was installed in 1883 and its console is now at the other side of the church.

Below: The church interior as it is today, facing east towards the altar.

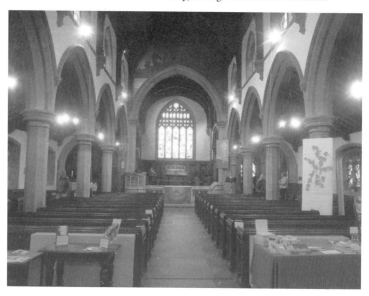

The renamed Brontë Chapel to the right of the altar. This quiet room contains relics from the former church.

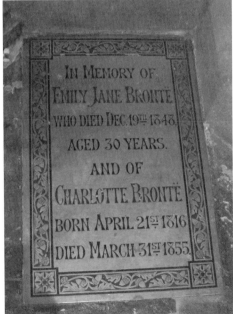

Brass plaque on the floor beside the Brontë Chapel which commemorates Emily and Charlotte.

Above: The beautiful old Communion table used for hundreds of years in the old church and now housed in the renamed Brontë Chapel.

Below: The marble memorial to the entire Brontë family on the chapel wall. Note that Anne Brontë is the only member of the family not buried below Haworth church. Her grave is in the area known as Paradise, in Scarborough. It is high above the town and below the castle, in the graveyard of St Mary's church.

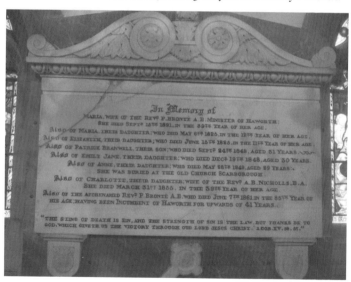

Above: The American Window, dedicated by an American admirer of Charlotte Brontë.

Right: A list of the church incumbents from 1654 to the present day. Patrick Brontë held the post for the longest time of 41 years.

Chapter 8

A guided walk around the graveyard at Haworth church

Walk 3

The graveyard surrounding the church of St Michael and All Angels at Haworth is very old and contains an estimated number of over 40,000 bodies in a very small area of around two acres. There were almost no regulations regarding burials until the twentieth century and graves were dug and re-dug many times over the centuries. Bodies could be piled up on top of each other many times and the sexton's job was a dangerous one, where holes in the earth and putrid decay were a constant hazard. There are crypts and vaults all over the graveyard and some have collapsed in on themselves over the years.

Before the closure of the graveyard the sloping earth drained water from the moors that ran through the graves and seeped into the drinking water. This unhealthy state of affairs existed during the Brontës' time and was the cause of many cases of cholera, typhus fever, and other killer epidemics. The important connection between contaminated water and disease was not confirmed until the mid- to late nineteenth century when Dr John Snow made the link between the cholera epidemic of 1848 in London and the drinking water at the Broad Street pump in Soho.

Other factors made this graveyard especially unpleasant. There was a lack of trees and foliage which normally help to aerate the ground and disperse gasses, and there was a habit of laying gravestones directly on to the ground or as table tops over the graves, which again prevented the circulation of air so necessary to speed decomposition and disperse odours. The ground on which the church stands also contained burials and had its own crypt and there was a time when people spoke of obnoxious fluids and gasses rising up from beneath the church floor; a feature of many, if not all, churches at some time in their history.

In his excellent book, *Ghosts and Gravestones of Haworth* the guide and writer Philip Lister describes graves of ten or twelve bodies deep in some parts of the graveyard. The whole of the hillside here must be riddled with holes, underground chambers and caved-in graves which means that visitors must be vigilant when venturing into the area.

Now overgrown with trees and bushes the graveyard is an atmospheric and romantic place full of sadness and yet calm and beautiful and it contains some very interesting graves and gravestones. This couple of intensely filled acres holds an historic record of the lives and deaths of the families who lived and died in and around Haworth over hundreds of years. The graveyard was finally closed in the mid-nineteenth century when a new Protestant cemetery was begun on the edge of Penistone Hill (see later walk).

The church graveyard was the background to the lives of the Brontë family and a constant reminder of life and death. They would have heard the bells every day of their lives and the constant tapping of the sextons hammer as he etched the names and dates onto the tombstones. They could not look out of the front windows or leave by the front door without the constant view of graves. Every funeral, and there were up to 200 each year, would be heralded by the tolling of the Passing Bell. This would be accompanied by the sound of horses' hooves on the cobblestones and the sight of mourners wending their way through the graveyard. Many funerals were followed by a wake in one of the four public houses at the top of Main Street and they were often noisy affairs despite the solemnity of the occasion. The sounds, sights and smells of these events were a backdrop to the lives of the local people but especially those living in such close proximity to the graves.

As with any graveyard, the oldest graves are in or around the church and gradually move outwards. Beneath the south wall of the church are the flat gravestones of some of the earliest graves and these may have once stood upright or been deliberately laid down to prevent grave robbery or being disturbed by scavenging animals. Some of the engraving is indecipherable but it is still possible to read names and dates from the 1600s. Many local names are found including Pighills, Ogdens, Robinsons and Uttleys. There will also have been unmarked paupers graves throughout the graveyard, often further away from the church itself as those closest to the church were mostly reserved for those who could pay for the privilege. Sometimes the same stone could be used more than once and for different families who could not afford a stone for themselves. There was also the practice of reselling graves after a family had died out and the plot would be resold and reused.

There are more flattened gravestones at the west side of the path that runs down to the south door of the church. These graves also date back to the 17th and 18th centuries and contain more local names. Here lie many of the Greenwood families, the Hartleys, Sunderlands and Rushworths; names often associated with local businessmen and reflecting the areas of agriculture and commerce. It is worth reading the inscriptions and noting the different ages and occupations of those interred.

Opposite the south side of the church and across the path leading down into the town is a section with mainly upright stones and amongst these, at the edge of the path, can be seen the original carved stone font presented to the church by William Grimshaw and used over the next 150 years. The Rev. William Grimshaw, the vicar at Haworth from 1742 to 1763, was a famous preacher who bullied and cajoled his congregation into attending church. He was a friend of John and Charles Wesley and agreed with their Evangelical Methodism which took the preacher out to the people. The Methodist revival and the Baptist ministry were accepted in

Haworth where a number of dissenting religions were popular. Both of the Wesley brothers preached in Haworth, out in the fields and from the three-decker pulpit.

Again local names appear on the gravestones and one sees Heatons, Ackroyds, Feathers and Sutcliffes. Not all stonemasons were adept at calligraphy and some may not have been able to read and often copied letters and numbers wrongly. Sometimes a family could afford decoration and paid for extra symbolic ornamentation. For example, an angel with open wings represented the flight of the soul; a weeping angel, grief; a dove, resurrection and innocence. Ivy represents friendship and fidelity; laurel leaves; immortality; a Celtic cross, eternity and a draped urn, immortality. There are many and these decorated tombstones demonstrate a large selection of them.

A particular grave in this area of the graveyard lies near to the back of The Black Bull public house and has only two initials and a date. The small stone reads, 'J S 1796'. This unique grave is that of James Sutcliffe, a local and violent highwayman who was hanged, following his trial at York Assizes, by the equally notorious hangman Jack Ketch. Somehow, Sutcliffe's body was smuggled back to Haworth and buried next to his favourite drinking place, probably by his friends and not with a Christian burial.

Also buried in this area of the churchyard is the doctor, John Wheelhouse who attended to Branwell Brontë and tried unsuccessfully to stop his alcohol addiction. Reading the various gravestone inscriptions informs you of the health of the population. Some show how multiple wives are buried with one man as each succumbed in turn to illness or died in childbirth. Many graves describe a number of children without names who all 'died in infancy'. One reads of the heartbreak of families who buried multiple children who never reached adolescence.

The graveyard was extended to the area below and beside the Parsonage probably around the end of the 1700s when more space was needed. A path runs up between the two sections to the south of the Parsonage. This area contains a number of interesting gravestones of famous local people. In this section one finds the grave of Timothy Feather, known as the last of the handloom weavers. Timothy Feather lived for all his long life in a weaver's cottage in the tiny hamlet of Buckley Green, a mile south of Stanbury amongst the moorlands (see later walk).

Timothy was born in January 1825 and was baptised by Patrick Brontë. He died in November 1910 after a lifetime of weaving. He lived a very frugal life and stayed at his loom for over seventy years. Philip Lister has calculated that during his weaving lifetime, Timothy Feather must have completed the weaving cycle of foot pedals and shuttle over 540 million times and woven around 235,000 yards of cloth! (See P. Lister Page 71). Timothy never married but became quite a celebrity and visitors began to call at his cottage to view his lifestyle and watch him work. His cottage was stuffed with all manner of objects and curiosities and when he died his loom and some of the contents of his home were removed to Cliffe Castle Museum in Keighley, where they can be seen today.

Very close to the path where it meets the north/south intersection with the path between Church Street and the route to Sowdens, (Rev. Grimshaw's original Parsonage home) there is a beautifully carved gravestone in memory of the children of Joseph and Elizabeth Heaton. Carved by their stonemason father, this gravestone and surround represents a child's crib and shows a sleeping infant curled up on a pillow and sheltered beneath the canopy headstone. Leaves and flowers are delicately cut into the stone which covers the grave of the seven Heaton children who did not survive infancy. Many people visit this sad monument to loss and appreciate the pain which their parents must have suffered.

There are graves around here that reflect the trades of the deceased. There is one with a musical score and others draped with cloth or with signs and symbols of the textile industry to which most of the townsfolk were connected. It is interesting to seek out these stones and others that record the lives and work of the families beneath.

The area immediately surrounding the Parsonage, on its south and east sides, holds the graves of many people known to the Brontës including the famous Barraclough clockmakers, the most notable with the dubious name of Zarubbabel Barraclough (1799–1878). Barraclough's clockmakers shop stood opposite The Black Bull public house and was there for many years. His brother also had a shop further down Main Street. Patrick Brontë owned a Barraclough longcase (grand-father) clock and it is that which one sees on the staircase in the Parsonage. This clock-making dynasty lasted for five generations until the business was finally sold in 1958.

Another poignant reminder of the hard times and high mortality rates is reflected on the gravestone of the Whittaker family. The parents are buried with their sixteen children, twelve of them unnamed, three who died before the age of 10 and a daughter who died aged 19 years. Their father died before his last daughter but the mother outlived her entire family.

It is interesting to note that some people did live very long lives at a time when life expectancy was so appallingly low. One sees gravestones recording people living well into their eighties and nineties. One wonders what kind of illness and pain they suffered during those long and often difficult years, before the advent of medical care and better living and working conditions.

Do not leave the part of the graveyard close to the south wall of the Parsonage without noting the gravestone of the Brown family; the sextons and servants who knew the Brontës intimately. Martha Brown served the Brontës for most of her life and later visited Arthur Nicholls in Ireland. Her father and brother, William and John Brown, were close friends and associates of the family, especially Patrick and Branwell.

In front of the Parsonage and on the east side of the graveyard wall is the grave of Tabitha Aykroyd another much loved and faithful servant of the Brontë family. Tabby died in February 1855 only a month before Charlotte. Tabby worked at the Parsonage for over thirty years and had a big influence on the family. She often talked to them about life in Haworth in the previous century and told them all stories of fairies and ghosts and life before the building of the many textile mills and the advent of industrialisation. She also liked to repeat much of the local gossip.

This walk has shown you the location of some interesting graves but you need to spend time on your own reading the inscriptions and wandering carefully amongst the stones and trees to get to know the stories of the people buried here. Nowadays the air is often filled with the sounds of noisy rooks who have nested in the trees and the many colourful hens that peck around in the undergrowth as their cockerel screeches in the background. Come here at different seasons and at different times of the day or night when it is calm and quiet to appreciate the light, the darkness, the beauty and the atmosphere of this special and sacred place.

Fact File – Walk 3: The Graveyard of Haworth church.

Start/Finish – Grid ref: SE 030 372

OS Maps: OL21 (1:25,000), Landranger 104 (1:50,000)

Entrance off Church Street, west of Main Street, Haworth.

Please make a donation, (inside church). Allow over an hour.

General Information – no toilets or refreshment facilities, (plenty of facilities close by around the town centre). Pay and display car parks short walk to the north. Take special care in the graveyard, the ground is uneven with horizontal slabs very slippery when damp. Naturally, please show respect for this consecrated ground and the graves of the deceased.

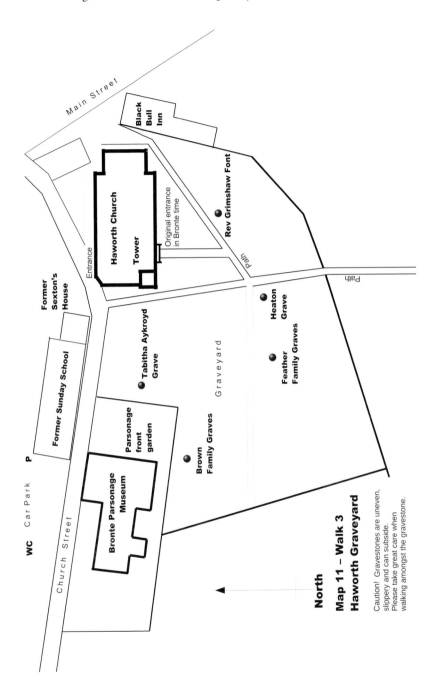

Main Street

Black Bull Inn

Haworth Church

Tower

Original entrance in Bronte time

Rev Grimshaw Font

Entrance

Former Sexton's House

Path

Path

Heaton Grave

Tabitha Aykroyd Grave

Feather Family Graves

Former Sunday School

Graveyard

P

Parsonage front garden

Brown Family Graves

WC   Car Park

Bronte Parsonage Museum

Church Street

North

Map 11 – Walk 3 Haworth Graveyard

Caution! Gravestones are uneven, slippery and can subside. Please take great care when walking amongst the gravestone.

Above: The flat gravestones on the south side of Haworth church.

Below: A pavement of gravestones under which many layers of bodies will have been interred.

The original font from the old church and used by Rev William Grimshaw and Patrick Brontë. It now stands open to the elements beside one of the graveyard paths, to the south of the church. In the background stands the Black Bull Inn. The east side of the graveyard borders on to the Inn and is where the highwayman, James Sutcliffe was secretly buried.

An example of gravestone decoration, often linked to the occupation of the deceased.

This large and beautifully carved memorial was created by stonemason Joseph Heaton in memory of seven of his children, who died in infancy.

Joseph Heaton's lovingly carved stone infant resting on a pillow under the shelter of the grave canopy. People often leave flowers here.

Above: In the south west part of the grave are many gravestones commemorating various members of the Feather family including Timothy Feather of Buckley Green, regarded as the last hand-loom weaver of the district.

Right: Near the south wall of the Parsonage stands the memorial to the Brown family. They were long time sextons of Haworth church and loyal servants and friends to the Brontë family. The house on Church Street adjoining the old Sunday school was built by John Brown and lived in by his family for many years.

Above: This plaque marks the original gateway in the garden wall where a path led to the church.

Below: The grave of Tabitha Aykroyd who served the Brontë family faithfully for over 30 years as both servant and friend.

Above left: The external, tiny door leading into the original part of the church tower containing the spiral staircase up to the roof.

Above right: The south facing sundial on the side of the church tower, dated 1726.

Below: A cat treads carefully along the north wall of the graveyard alongside Church Street.

Chapter 9

Penistone Hill Country Park and the new Haworth cemetery circular

Walk 4

Like many of the walks in this book, this one can begin in the centre of Haworth, or using one of the many car parks close to the Parsonage, or public transport. There is also a large car parking area on Penistone Hill itself. The walk can be anything from a circular stroll of little more than two kilometres, or extended by meandering around Penistone Country Park and visiting the 'new' cemetery.

Commence your ramble from outside of The Black Bull hotel and the front of St Michael and All Angles Church, on Main Street. Walk along the short passage beside the church to the north side, heading towards The Brontë Parsonage. You are now in Church Street and passing the Sexton's house and the old Sunday school buildings, erected in 1832. Note the plaque over the doorway. The Parsonage is to your left as you continue westward. Keep walking beyond the end of Church Street, still heading due-west along a well-defined path. Go through the gate and cross an open field. There are some paving stones but they are worn and very slippery in wet weather. Walk to the far right corner, where there is an iron kissing gate, and meet the top of West Lane, where you need to take care of road traffic.

Keep heading west and take the aptly named Cemetery Road, which is the left fork, as the main road bears right and becomes Sun Lane. You will pass on your left the junction with Dimples Lane. Continue on Cemetery Road and after a few hundred metres, the cemetery is to your left, protected from the harsh Pennine winds by a sturdy stone wall. The main entrance to the cemetery is another hundred metres along the road although there is an iron gate that also gives access at this point.

This cemetery was consecrated following the enforced closure of Haworth church graveyard on public health grounds sometime after the damming Babbage report, in the later part of the nineteenth century. It is an attractive space containing some beautiful stonework. Note again the familiar names of local families and the wonderful 'Bloomer Toothill', in the north-west corner. Some of the graves are in a stepped fashion which is unusual and have a slab depicting the various generations of a particular family.

As you walk into the graveyard you see to your immediate right the grave of Lily Cove, (Elizabeth Mary Cove) parachutist. This young lady was the main attraction at the Haworth Co-op Gala in the summer of 1906. She flew over Scar Top on a trapeze hung below a huge balloon. When she jumped, her parachute failed to open and she was killed. The people of Haworth raised money for her burial and the erection of the stone you see before you.

Compare the spacious and uniformed layout of this cemetery in stark contrast to the church graveyard at Haworth. The raised hillside and many trees offer an attractive and airy space and views over the Worth valley to the north. We suggest that you spend some time in this lovely setting and view the many interesting headstones.

When you have visited here, or if you do not wish to do so, you can now gain height up to Penistone Hill. Although there are many well defined paths, this is all 'open access land' so you can roam at your leisure.

The Country Park has several car parks, should you wish to avoid the walk from the town centre. The highest point is 314 metres and commands a good panoramic view of the Haworth area. The remains of quarry workings are visible and would have been the source of building materials for many structures in the vicinity and beyond.

To make your ramble circular, head east from Penistone Hill towards Dimples Lane. Another long-abandoned quarry is visible to your left, though nature has taken the harshness from the quarry slopes. Make your way over Dimples Lane and along the narrow track leading to Jagger's Quarry. This has been landscaped to form Weaver's Hill car park and is surrounded by mature trees. You can continue on your way via Weaver's Hill to Sun Lane, where you turn left to walk back towards Main Street and the steep climb back to The Black Bull and the church.

Alternatively, you can skirt around the Jagger's Quarry area, again on a well-marked footpath, towards the old graveyard that surrounds the south and west side of St Michael and All Angels Church. Fork right and you are back to the front of the church and outside The Black Bull, ready for a drink!

Not a long walk, but a pleasant way to spend a few hours on defined paths to the west of the town; routes and paths on which the Brontë children must have walked on hundreds of occasions and in all weathers.

The quarries in this area were owned and run by local wealthy mill owners, gentry and farmers and were another source of employment for the local people. There was an enormous demand for stone as the Industrial age advanced and more and more buildings were needed for industry, business and housing, and the stone construction of highways and bridges. Hundreds of men were needed in the quarries around Haworth which produced hardy Millstone Grit and Yorkshire Stone vital for the building of new towns and cities all over the country. There was only a limited use of gunpowder and in an era before mechanisation this was arduous and dangerous work. All the stone had to be cut and dressed by hand and carried by horse and cart.

Low grade coal was also mined in the area but the other major task was the cutting and drying of peat, as the town's major source of fuel. This was another task which employed many labourers and was a long and back-breaking chore.

When you wander over this area in the sunshine of a pleasant summer's day try and recall the hustle and bustle of hundreds of men cutting and hauling stone and the many horses and equipment used every day to manipulate and carry the heavy cargo. With simple tools and no Health and Safety rules it must, especially in the cold and bad weather, have been a difficult and dangerous place to work.

Fact File – Walk 4: Penistone Hill Country Park and the New Haworth cemetery Circular.

Start/Finish – Grid ref: SE 030 372

OS Maps: OL21 (1:25,000), Landranger 104 (1:50,000)

Start/finish on Church Street, Main Street, Haworth

General Information – no steep hills, but some moorland walking, 2–3km, allow 1–2 hours. Plus an hour in the graveyard.

Plenty of facilities close by in the town centre, along with pay and display car parks. Take special care in the graveyard, the ground can be uneven and, naturally, please show respect for this consecrated ground and the graves of the deceased.

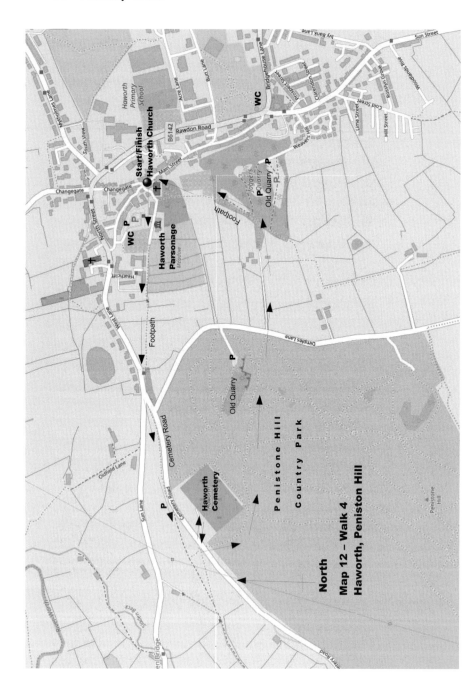

Above: The National Church Sunday school. This building was instigated by Patrick Brontë who sought grants and public subscription and saw it erected in 1832. The two gable ends at the West side were added later. Branwell and his sisters all taught here with varying success.

Below left: Plaque above the Sunday school door. It was, and still is, used for various events and functions.

Below right: The path at the west end of Church Street leading out across to the moors.

Above: Haworth 'new' municipal cemetery. There are lovely views across the valley from this charming and attractive place.

Left: The headstone erected by the people of Haworth to the memory of Lily Cove, the parachutist who died on Haworth Moor during the summer gala of June 1906, aged only 21 years.

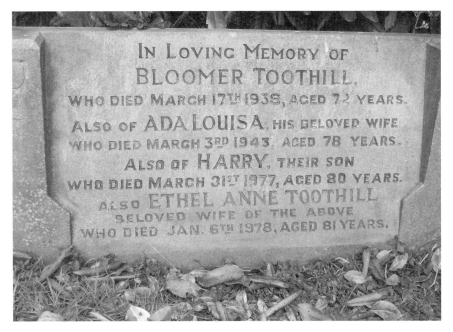

In Loving Memory of
BLOOMER TOOTHILL,
WHO DIED MARCH 17TH 1938, AGED 72 YEARS.
ALSO OF ADA LOUISA, HIS BELOVED WIFE
WHO DIED MARCH 3RD 1943, AGED 78 YEARS.
ALSO OF HARRY, THEIR SON
WHO DIED MARCH 31ST 1977, AGED 80 YEARS.
ALSO ETHEL ANNE TOOTHILL
BELOVED WIFE OF THE ABOVE
WHO DIED JAN. 6TH 1978, AGED 81 YEARS.

The grave of the oddly named Bloomer Toothill!

These photographs highlight the
stepped stonework of some of the
graves. An unusual feature which we
have not seen before in the area.

Above: A rough, stone road runs south off Cemetery Road up the hillside and was used by the quarrymen for transporting stone down from the quarry by horse and cart.

Below: Way marker for Penistone Country Park.

Above: Path leading down from the old quarry workings on Penistone Hill towards Haworth.

Below: One of your possible routes back to Haworth crossing Dimples Lane and along this narrow track leading to the former Jagger's Quarry which is now Weaver's Hill Car Park.

Chapter 10

A circular guided tour of Haworth town centre

Walk 5

To appreciate Haworth from around and after the era of the Brontës, we suggest that you walk from the north end of the town down through West Lane, Main Street, Bridgehouse Lane and Lees Lane to the train station and back up through the Haworth Central Park and return to the top of the town via the Rawdon Road bypass.

Begin your walk at The Old Sun Inn on the road referred to as West Lane which travels through the town and on to Stanbury to the north-west. This is the first of the many inns which served the community; not only of locals but travellers and drovers who regularly passed through the town en route between the mills of Yorkshire and Lancashire. West Lane was a turnpike road and part of the thread of roads that ran through Haworth as part of the Blue Bell Turnpike which connected Bradford to Colne in Lancashire. The tolls from travellers were collected at various buildings along the way. The Sun Inn was a staging post for horses and travellers and was the last hostelry serving the town before embarking across the moors and the first to be arrived at coming from Stanbury or the moorland routes.

Walking back towards Haworth, immediately on your left are two of the chapels built for the non-conformist population; Protestants who did not follow the established Church of England included Methodists, Wesleyans and Baptists amongst the dissenters. Here one sees the site of the West Lane Methodist Chapel which was built in 1758 and rebuilt in 1846. However, it was later demolished and the school building which stood beside the chapel has been used by the congregation since 1853. It has a graveyard at the rear. Patrick Brontë was not against different religious beliefs and worked together with many ministers from differing churches and chapels.

The next building is the West Lane Baptist Chapel. This was founded in the 1750s and the chapel built in 1844; it is used today by its congregation and hosts many Brontë Society events.

Cross the road outside of the Chapel and join the continuation of West Lane, which leads into Main Street. Over the centuries and also in connection with the Rawdon Road by-pass, street names in Haworth have altered. The street you are now entering is known as both West Lane and Main Street and leads to the small square at the top of the main road through Haworth. You will see many houses and terraces here that date from the eighteenth and nineteenth centuries. A few are even earlier. One row on your left are back-to-back cottages with former cellar dwellings. Further along to your right you will see a small square known as The Fold. In 1851 over fifty people were living in these few houses and their overcrowding and appalling sanitation must have made their lives very difficult. As you view these places try not to see them through modern-day eyes, but imagine them 200 years ago and the sights, sounds and events that must have coloured the lives of the inhabitants.

Continue along to the end of West Lane where you will see The Old White Lion inn on your left and The Kings Arms inn on your right. Both of these inns have stood here for over 300 years. A noticeboard on your right will give you some of the history of The King's Arms, a former seventeenth-century Manor House, and information on its function in the nineteenth century as an inn, a slaughterhouse and a mortuary. The front entrance faces Church Street and a short walk up the lane reveals the church and graveyard and the Brontë Parsonage Museum.

The imposing Yorkshire stone front of the Old White Lion faces onto the small square at the top of Main Street. The Inn was remodelled and extended in 1858. Again one finds an old inn full of charm and hospitality that has served the community for hundreds of years.

Adjoining The Old White Lion is the current Haworth Information Centre. This building was used by the Mechanics Institute after its foundation in 1849 but was superseded by the Yorkshire Penny Bank in 1894. The building of the short tower and the pyramid-shaped roof were added at this time. The first floor of this building held the small but burgeoning collection of Brontë relics held by the Brontë Society, founded in 1893, and became their first museum before the move to the Parsonage in 1928. The building stands at the junction of West Lane and Changegate. A short wander down Changegate lane reveals more stone cottages built in the eighteenth and nineteenth centuries. The Information Centre also faces onto 'The Square', an area with no official title but known by this name and surrounded by shops and inns.

This area is of great interest and was the core of the town in the time of the Brontës. Many of the buildings are of eighteenth-century origin and they included another hostelry, The Cross Inn, which stood on the site of the current post office and adjoining shop. These four inns all surrounding the square, The Black Bull, The Cross Inn, The King's Arms and The Old White Lion had the addition of a Temperance Hall in their midst. This was housed in the three storeyed house at 123 Main Street. Patrick Brontë was President of the Haworth Temperance Society and, ironically, Branwell was for a time, one of its members.

The shop at number 121 Main Street, between the former Temperance Hall and the church steps has belonged to the Hartley family for generations. Arthur Hartley was a Chairman of The Brontë Society during the 1980s and a very active supporter. He died in his late nineties in August 2010 and the house and shop are still kept by one of his daughters. This is typical of a town where generations of the same family continue over long periods and unlike so many, do not disperse and move on from their roots and traditions. William Hartley, (1792–1868) ran the Post Office from this shop between

1830 and 1857 and it is from here that the Brontës would have posted and collected, their letters and manuscripts.

The Black Bull inn, which stands at the other side of the church steps, was Branwell's favourite drinking place and it is said that he had his own chair where he would regale passing travellers and local drinkers with his oratory skills. This inn, like the other three, was a welcome hostelry for travellers and their horses over many years and was an important and thriving part of the town. Many business meetings and committees met in these hostelries and still do. The remaining three inns still welcome and provide for locals and tourists alike. All three house restaurants and offer bed and breakfast to visitors.

Another notable building on this square is the Old Apothecary, recently renamed, Cabinet of Curiosities. This former druggist shop still retains its furnishings from its time as a chemists where all drugs were stored and weighed out to customers. In the time of the Brontës, opium was sold over the counter in much the same way as alcohol or tobacco is today. Opium is a narcotic which, when mixed with alcohol, creates laudanum, a drug used frequently to alleviate pain and induce sleep. It was used throughout the nineteenth century as a remedy for most ailments including those of children and, with few alternatives, many people became addicted. A walk around this shop today offers another nostalgic reminder of the past.

Moving on to the top of the steep Main Street there is a lovely view of the slope down into the valley and the distant hills above and beyond Haworth to the south-east. Immediately to your left is an archway. This charming passage once led to the area known as Gauger's Croft and the premises of a thriving wines and spirits trade mainly owned and run by the Thomas family. Many houses were also situated here on the steep bank side which became known as Brandy Row.

When Benjamin Babbage came to Haworth to conduct his survey and produce his famous report on the health and sanitation of the town in the 1850s, he was particularly concerned with the appalling conditions for the residents of this area. Many were wool combers who had to keep their houses unbearably hot and humid in order to treat the wool, so there was little or no ventilation. These conditions were ideal for the spreading of diseases and the cause of poor health and early deaths especially from conditions of the lungs. The romantic view today hides a wealth of misery and hard labour.

Some alarming figures for Haworth were produced by Mr Babbage in his report to the General Board of Health. They included the following statistics:

There were 69 toilets for 2,500 people

24 Houses shared one toilet. Another seven houses had no toilet at all.

One cellar dwelling had a family of seven who slept in two beds.

41.6% of the babies born never reached the age of six.

There were no sewers, just covered drains, but most refuse ran along open gutters.

The death rate for Haworth was 44.3% more than that of the neighbouring villages.

Extracts from the Babbage Report 1850

Turning back into Main Street and continuing down the steep slope of the road notice the cobbles, or setts, which were laid sideways to help horses gain a footing as they hauled people and goods up and down the street. Until the by-pass was built in the late 1970's, all transport and goods came up and down this thoroughfare, including buses!

Two hundred years ago there were the added hazards of rubbish, night soil, horse dung and other effluence covering the cobblestones. Most people kept domestic pets as well as pigs, geese and chickens, to add to the melee. Dr Wheelhouse and Patrick Brontë both petitioned for a government agent to come and see for themselves the lack of a pure water supply and the appalling sanitation, but their pleas went unheeded for many months. Eventually Benjamin Herschel Babbage arrived from the General Board of Health in April 1850 and was shocked by a town which had one of the highest mortality rates in the country. Conditions in places were worse than those of the slums in the east end of London. His subsequent report included the recommendation to immediately close the graveyard as one of the sources of water pollution.

As you continue downwards note a ginnel (West Yorkshire name for a narrow alleyway, or snickett) on your right named Lodge Street. This narrow way, or court, formerly named Newell Hill, was the site of the Masonic Lodge attended by Branwell Brontë. The Lodge of the Three Graces of Ancient, Free and Accepted Masons came to Haworth in 1806. After twenty years of meetings at The Black Bull inn it was housed in rooms above number 9 in what became Lodge Street and was accessed by an outside staircase which can still be seen. It leads from what is now a most charming courtyard, but one has to imagine it 200 years ago.

Also visible is the former home and premises of William Wood the carpenter who was often employed by Patrick Brontë and who produced coffins as well as furniture and did general repairs. He made all the coffins for the Brontë burials and much of their furniture. His detached house shows an outside stone staircase which led to his workshop. William was the great-nephew of the Brontë servant, Tabitha Aykroyd and they owned a cottage in this tiny street. William had fourteen children and his was only one of a group of around fifteen families who lived in this tiny space along with their animals. Some of the cottages housed wool combers and, again, the heat and foul air would have affected all those living here.

It is hard for us to imagine the overcrowding and the living conditions of people in these areas and yet, as noted, alongside the seriously high mortality rates a few people managed to live well into old age. This was an amazing achievement in a world with no antibiotics, no labour-saving machinery and no decent sanitation or clean drinking water. Even today this little ginnel feels claustrophobic but is a delight for lovers of social history, as is Main Street itself, as a living reminder of the lives and movement of people and animals over centuries.

As you continue downhill you are seeing the houses and cottages that have been here, with others before them, since before the Brontë family arrived in 1820. Hundreds of people lived and worked on this street. There were many businesses, especially butchers, grocers and wine merchants, and many cottage industries, mainly wool combing. Today it is alive with tea shops, souvenir and clothes shops and caters for a huge population of tourists. In an area where people once died of hunger it is impossible to avoid an enormous range of food and drink establishments.

The number of inns indicates the amount of business and passing trade and travel which occurred in this one street and another inn now presents itself on your right-hand side.

The Fleece Inn was built in the late eighteenth century here at 67 Main Street and has been a hostelry since that time. Like all the inns in Haworth it offers bed and breakfast and hearty, home-cooked food. Opposite the Fleece Inn is the start of Butt Lane, formally providing an access to the back of some of the many back-to-back dwellings it also now leads down to the railway station.

As Main Street widens you are seeing an area that has changed over the last 150 years and would not be recognisable to a visitor before that time. To your left was open space in the 1800s with small gardens and animal sheds where now are various new buildings. On your right cottages and shops have been built and rebuilt over the years. The Haworth Industrial Co-operative Society moved to their new Central Stores here in 1897 and can be seen in the large three-storeyed purpose built premises on your right. To your left, on the corner of Main Street, is the building that was the original Old Registry office.

You are now at the junction with the bypass (Rawdon Road) leading from Bridgehouse Lane, sometimes referred to as Brighouse Lane. There are public toilets in Haworth Park on the opposite side of Rawdon Road. To your right is Sun Street, an area that is worth a walk around. Immediately to your right is one of the oldest houses in Haworth, Haworth Old Hall; another attractive and welcoming hostelry.

The Old Hall dates back to around 1580 when it was built as a large Manor House. The history of the Hall is not well documented and it has had many uses over the centuries. It was bought by the Emmott family in the eighteenth century who did not live there but rented it out to various people for various uses. It was known as Emmott Hall at this time. It has been a farm and was also divided into separate dwellings or tenements by another absentee landlord, Major General Edward Green-Emmott-Rawdon of Rawdon Hall. It is a pleasure to see it now returned to its former glory; it is a beautiful building and well worth a visit.

Across the road from The Old Hall and standing at the corner of Sun Street and Bridgehouse Lane, is the Hall Green Baptist Chapel. Established in the 1820s this chapel was a breakaway faction from the other Baptist establishment at West Lane Baptist Chapel. Both chapels had slightly different religious views and both were dominated by branches of the Greenwood family of mill owners. The rich employers in Haworth influenced their workforce and encouraged church attendance. There was a definite link between church and business and on the building or demolishing of different churches and chapels. As the fortunes of the rich waxed and waned so did the church congregations. Consequently, the Church of England had less support at times than the dissenting churches, depending on which land and mill owner had the most influence. There is a small and interesting graveyard here.

Continue down Bridgehouse Lane to the bridge over the railway line and look to your right to see the mill belonging to the Greenwood family in the time of the Brontës. Their house is to the left of the mill amongst the trees and is now a delightful bed and breakfast hotel. Mills needed to have a water supply and you can see the Bridgehouse Beck running alongside the rail track.

Turning left into Station Road, walk along passed the railway sidings, which contain a variety of rolling stock from the last century. The main workshops are based at Ingrow station, near to Keighley. Stay on your left until you reach Haworth station and then go into the station and have a look around. This railway from Keighley to Oxenhope was opened in April 1867 and you can visit all of its six stations on your walks. Oakworth station was the setting for the famous film *The Railway Children* adapted from the book by Edith Nesbitt. A ride on the restored Keighley and Worth Valley Railway is a treat and a wonderful way to see the Worth valley and experience travel in the time of the steam train.

Further details of the history, closure and rebirth of the Worth Valley Railway are in chapter 18. The present layout of Haworth Station dates from improvements made along the railway in the 1880s, when it was remodelled to cater for the increase in traffic throughout the route. With so many mills along the line of the railway, traffic quickly developed and services were increased significantly.

Even if you are not taking the train, time can be spent looking around this beautifully kept station. If you are lucky enough to be there during one of the many steam days, then you can easily imagine you are in the 1930s. Numerous enamelled advertising signs adorn the station walls and fences. Gas lanterns extend over the length of the platform. Inside the building is a well-stocked shop with limited refreshments which help to fund the work of volunteers who maintain and operate the railway. Toilets are also located at the station, which is built on a long curve with just one platform adjoining the station buildings. Please purchase a platform ticket if you venture beyond the station shop.

To continue your circular walk, turn right out of the station buildings and take the path that leads onto the footbridge and over the railway line. A good view of the sidings is afforded from the footbridge, before continuing to Butt Lane. This is a steep cobbled road, so do take care if the surface is wet. You can take the path through Haworth Central Park on your left if you wish. The Park is well maintained with many gardens, a children's playing area and an ornate bandstand as the centre piece. This recreational space is regularly used by residents and tourist alike and was developed in the 1920s. You may prefer to continue directly up Butt Lane and reach Rawdon Road from this route.

Rawdon Road runs parallel with Main Street and forms a bypass to the cobbled town centre street. Take the bypass and climb the gentle slope of the tree lined road towards the north of the town, with the modern school buildings of Haworth Primary School, on your right.

It was only in the last 40 years, with the building of the by-pass, that relief was brought to the town centre and the steep Main Street. In stark contrast, traffic now runs freely as Rawdon Road takes you sweeping round a bend to the West.

Changegate meets this road on the left at the top of the curve and there is another public car park on your left, where once dozens of former slum houses, were squashed back-to-back. The road now becomes North Street. On your right is Townend Farm, one of the oldest building in Haworth and dating back to about 1600. Of an unusual design for this area; it has a gable that lies at a right-angle to the main body of the house and you can still identify many of the original stone features. Beside the house and to the east are the old barns which originally housed part of Rushworth Lund's Mill.

Pass West Lane Baptist Chapel on your right-hand side and The Old Sun Inn is just a little further to the left. A most interesting circular walk that takes in so much of the historic past of Haworth. The town is now bustling with tourists from all over the world who come to find and admire a town that holds an amazing social and literary history. We feel that it is important to remember and appreciate the lives of the many who lived here and toiled in the unhealthy conditions that limited their harsh and difficult lives.

Fact File – Walk 5: Circular guided tour of Haworth town centre.

Start/Finish – Grid ref: SE 027 374

OS Maps: OL21 (1:25,000), Landranger 104 (1:50,000)

Start/finish The Old Sun Inn, West Lane, Haworth

General Information – a few steep hills, but all firm walking, 1-2km, allow 1-2 hours. Plenty of facilities all along the route through the town and car parks at West Street, Changegate, or leave Main Street and turn up Sun Street to access Weaver's Hill Car Park. For railway passengers there is limited parking at Haworth Railway station.

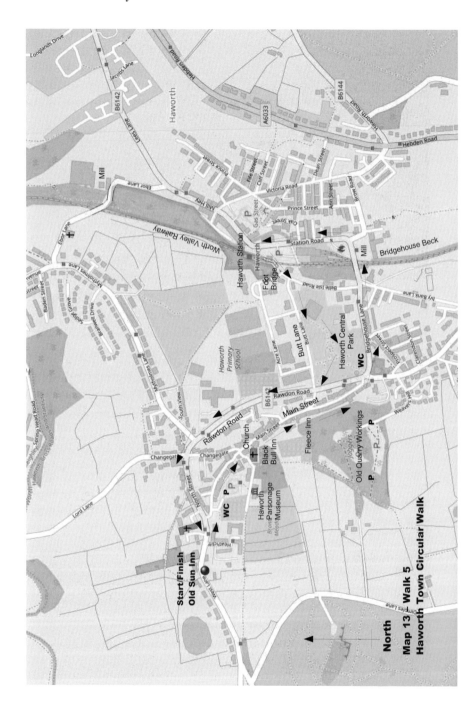

Start/Finish
Old Sun Inn

North

Map 13 Walk 5
Haworth Town Circular Walk

Above: The Old Sun Inn on the ancient toll road leading out of Haworth to the north west of the town and the start of this circular walk.

Below: The school building of the former West Lane Methodist Chapel which was built in 1758. The Chapel was later demolished and this building has been used by the congregation since 1853.

Above: West Lane
Baptist Chapel. This
chapel was built in 1844
and is still in use.

Left: Interesting feature
on a house roof in West
Lane.

Above: The street sign of The Fold.

Below: The Fold on the right of West Lane going towards the top of Main Street. It was once inhabited by 50 families and their animals. Note the former communal 'privvies' in the background.

Above: The Old White Lion Inn which has been altered and added to over its long history but remains a welcoming hostelry.

Left: Likewise, The Kings Arms offers food and accommodation. This lovely old Inn and its history is described on a board on its north-west facing, outside wall.

Right: Standing between West Lane and Change gate is the current Tourist Information Office. It was formerly the Mechanics Institute and then the Yorkshire Penny Bank. It housed the original Brontë Museum collection on the first floor, before the Parsonage was donated to the Brontë Society in 1928 by Sir James Roberts.

Below: Recently renamed the 'Cabinet of Curiosities', this building is the former Apothecary where a range of drugs was available to treat all manner of diseases.

Above: A lovely picture of the beautiful interior of the former apothecary showing some of the original display cabinets.

Below: The Black Bull Inn, the fourth hostelry on this walk and a favourite drinking den of Branwell's and a centre of village life and business.

Above left: Looking from Main Street one sees the archway of Gauger's Croft. This archway formally led to the warehouses of many wine merchants and the infamous overcrowded housing of Brandy Row.

Above right: Gauger's Croft from the South looking towards Main Street. Gauger is the old name for the excise men who examined the goods and collected taxes.

A typical ginnel or snicket running between the premises on Main Street.

Above: Lodge Street with William Wood's house and workshop. He worked for many years in his joiners shop at the top of the stairs. Here he made furniture and coffins for the local people, including the Brontë family.

Below: A delightful view from the inside of Lodge Street looking north. It shows the stone steps leading up to the former rooms of The Lodge of the Three Graces of Ancient, Free and Accepted Masons, of which Branwell Brontë was once a member.

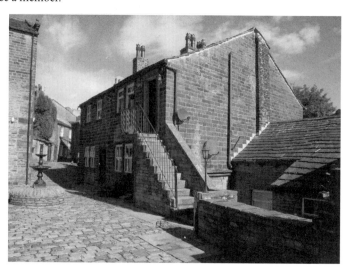

Above: Moving down Main Street amongst the shops and business premises that have always dominated this busy thoroughfare.

Right: Another example of a quaint ginnel.

Above: The Fleece Inn. The fifth hostelry on our walk and another welcoming inn that has served the community for over 200 years.

Below: Old Midland style railway sign pointing down towards Haworth station.

Above left: Continuing to the bottom of Main Street where the old co-op building still stands on the right, beside cottages built after the Brontës' time.

Above right: Cottages on Main Street.

Below: The building that housed the former Haworth registrars' offices.

Above: At the junction of Main Street and Sun Street stands one of the town's oldest buildings, The Old Hall. This is now also a hostelry offering food and accommodation.

Left: Opposite the Old Hall and facing Bridgehouse Lane is Hall Green Methodist Chapel. Built in 1820 it includes a small, neat graveyard with many interesting memorial stones.

Above: Opposite the chapel is now Haworth's recreational park. A delightful area in which to sit or play, with beautiful and well-tended gardens.

Below: Continuing to the bottom of Bridgehouse Lane you walk across the railway bridge with the Keighley to Oxenhope line below you. To your right is the former Bridgehouse Mill, built and owned by the Greenwood family, and which is currently being converted into flats.

Above: A view from Bridgehouse Lane railway bridge looking left into the railway siding workshops at some immaculate steam locomotives being prepared for duties.

Left: Crossing the footbridge above Haworth Station, you have a fine view of a train about to depart for Keighley.

Above: As you climb up Rawdon Road you reach the junction with Changegate and Rawdon Road becomes North Street. To your right are the remaining buildings of the former Rushworth Lund's Mill.

Below: This lovely building is known as Townend Farm and dates back to the 1600's. Note the gable end at right angles to the main house. Continue on North Street, re-passing the chapels on your right and return to your starting point at The Old Sun Inn.

Chapter 11

Haworth circular to Oxenhope and Field Head

Walk 6

This is an excellent walk for those who do not like to stray too far from the villages and, like most of the walks in this book, gives many options for you to reduce or extend the overall distance, should the weather be changeable. Throughout its length it is never far from the railway line and the valley of the Bridgehouse Beck, so you do not need to be an avid map reader to follow the route.

With car parks to the west and north of Haworth town centre, you will start this walk from the south end of Main Street. You need to be heading due east along Bridgehouse Lane, down the steep hill towards the bridge over the beck and the railway line. If you have arrived by train, alight at Haworth station, then a short walk out of the station yard, turning right (south) along Station Road to where it meets Bridgehouse Lane and the War Memorial.

At this junction of Station Road, Bridgehouse Lane and Brow Road, you need to turn south and walk just a short distance along Brow Road. Bridgehouse Mill and the house of the former mill owner, John Greenwood, is on your right as you cross over into Brow Road. As the road turns left, there is a public footpath sign on your right, taking you away from the road.

You can now enjoy two kilometres of paths taking you from Haworth to Oxenhope. The route is generally flat, though can be a little muddy after heavy rain. To your right is both the railway line and the Bridgehouse Beck. Hebden Road, which is the A6033, is on the higher ground not far to the east, but far enough away to keep you in a tranquil setting. Some further development work is spreading along the valley, but essentially it is a lovely countryside route.

With many options to reduce your route back, two paths leave the main route to the right. These can lead you over the beck and under the railway, and back into Haworth via Marsh Lane Top and Sun Street. To stay on the main route, do not cross the beck, but keep walking south. A number of paths also lead to the east, taking you up to Hebden Road, but again, stay on the main route south.

The beck takes a meandering course but where the railway bends away from the river, you finally do cross over the beck and steadily walk closer to the railway lines. With the start of the sidings and workshops of the Worth Valley Railway's station at Oxenhope, you can take another option to cross over the railway on a 'barrow crossing' (a level foot crossing without gates) and head north-west, reducing the length of the walk by a kilometre. We suggest remaining on the main path heading generally south, which permits you to view the station and museum at Oxenhope, or walk a little further into the village centre.

Oxenhope was so close to Haworth that the Brontës would all have walked over to it and enjoyed the surrounding countryside. Oxenhope is a village scattered over an area where there are clusters of separate dwellings and communities. It is divided into the Lower and Upper town areas and that around the railway station. Like Haworth, it stood on an old turnpike road and it had its share of mills and millworkers' houses, and several churches and chapels. Oxenhope church is worth a visit. It was built in 1849 with the enthusiasm of its first vicar, the Rev. Joseph Grant who was in sympathy with Patrick Brontë over the need to raise funds for national schools. Like the Rev. Brontë he did much to assist his parishioners in their health and education. Many of the mills were demolished in the last century, often following major fires, a huge hazard in these buildings. Perseverance mill began life as Lowertown Methodist Chapel in 1805 which became too small for its congregation. The mill took over and was extended but was finally demolished in 1990 following a fire, but the burial ground can still be seen. The road running south through the centre of the village winds up past Sykes mill and on to Leeming Wells and over the moor top to Denholme. Again, a series of public houses stood along the turnpike road and some are still doing trade today and are worth a visit just to see their old interiors and solid construction.

At the road, turn west (right) and walk into the main station car park. Some refreshments are available here, when the train services are operating. As with all the stations along the Worth valley route, Oxenhope station is immaculately kept by the volunteers and can be a hive of activity in the summer months. Apart from the interesting station buildings and surround, the engine shed to your right houses a small museum for the enthusiasts to spend time mulling over. You have the option to return by train, or indeed, start/finish your walk here.

Continuing the walk, come out of the station and turn right along Mill Lane to the junction with Moorhouse Lane (to the right). You will now be heading almost due north for a few hundred metres (take care of road traffic) before turning right again at the footpath sign. The path heads north-east for a few hundred metres before coming to a crossroad of paths.

The path to your right leads back to cross under the railway, where you could have taken a short cut. The path ahead provides a slightly shorter route back to Haworth, but we suggest that you turn left here towards Marsh Lane. In a few hundred metres the lane is reached and you should turn left for just a short section on the road, before turning right again into Old Oxenhope Lane.

It is another few hundred metres before the road turns sharp left, but you turn off to your right, back onto field paths. This elevated stretch of the walk enables you to look across the valley with Haworth laid out before you. This also forms part of the Brontë way footpath and passes close to Field Head Farm. Several paths lead down to Sun Street in

Haworth, but stay on the main path which eventually meets another at right angles. Here you do turn right and back towards Haworth.

You can walk down to the village via the large car park at Weavers Hill, or continue towards and through the graveyard surrounding the church. Whichever way you choose, you are back in the bustle of Haworth centre ready to return to your transport or a much-needed refreshment break.

A very pleasant circular walk of around five kilometres (three miles) if you have followed the full route, so taking you around two hours when taking in the views and points of interest.

Fact File – Walk 6: Haworth circular to Oxenhope and Field Head.

Start/Finish – Grid ref: SE 030 373

OS Maps: OL21 (1:25,000), Landranger 104 (1:50,000)

Start/finish The Black Bull Inn, Main Street, Haworth.

A few steep hills and field paths, all well signed, 5km, allow over 2 hours.

General Information – plenty of facilities around Haworth town and at Oxenhope station. Pay and display car parks around Haworth town and also at the railway stations (though these are for people using the trains). Parts of the route can be muddy after wet weather, so boots are advisable, as it is not always possible to avoid deep puddles on parts of the route.

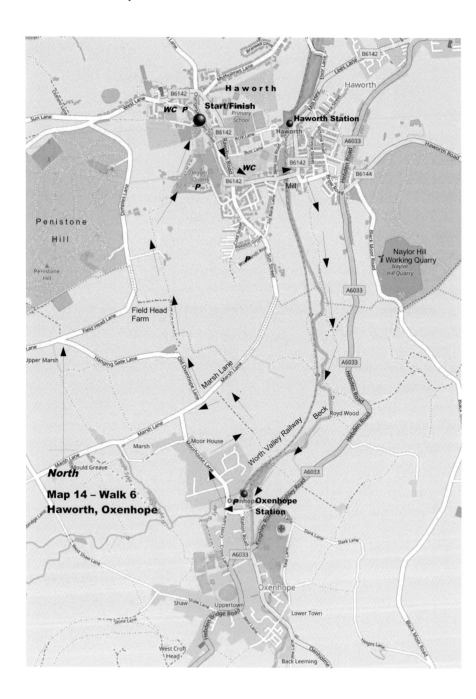

The grade 2 listed Georgian 'Bridge House', the former home of the Greenwood family. They also built and owned the adjoining Bridgehouse Mills.

You need to look carefully to spot the way marker footpath sign, leading you through the narrow gap at the start of your walk to Oxenhope.

Above and below: Two delightful views of a typical stone bridge over the beck with a further iron Girder Bridge taking the railway over the footpath, mid-way between Haworth and Oxenhope. This route can be taken if you wish to shorten your walk.

Above: A typical view of the delightful path that takes you along the east side of Bridgehouse Beck for 2km to Oxenhope.

Below: Another footbridge can take you over the beck and then the railway, just a short distance from Oxenhope Station and Carriage Sheds.

Above: Many small streams cross the route of your path to Oxenhope, the more substantial ones being bridged to keep your boots dry!

Below: The well-kept Oxenhope Station and wonderful flower beds, lovingly tendered by volunteers. Midland Railway red is the prominent colour of all the station fixtures.

Above: Another view of Oxenhope Station looking north towards Haworth.

Below: This view of Oxenhope Station looks south towards the buffer stop and single column water tower. The railway track to the right enables the locomotive crew that have pulled the train into the station from Keighley, to 'run around' their train and pull it from the other end, back to Haworth and Keighley.

Above: So typical of the narrow paths with stone flags around this part of West Yorkshire. Note: the smooth stone flags can be very slippery when wet!

Below: Part of the route back to Haworth you occupy the higher ground, well above the railway and the beck, to the east. You have clear views of the town to the north east.

Above: Views over Haworth to the east as you near the church and graveyard.

Below: Looking back at the path on the left where you have returned from Oxenhope, you proceed straight on, passed the path west leading to Penistone Hill.

Chapter 12

A wild walk to Top Withins

Walks 7 and 8

Of all the walks in this book, a trek over the moors offers a better understanding of how and why this wild location inspired the Brontë sisters in their writing projects. Like the poet William Wordsworth, the Brontë children saw education and learning from nature, as an equal to that of both books and religion. Nature spoke to their emotions and their senses and as you walk in their footsteps you will feel the effects of this beautiful landscape.

The location of Withins Height, and Top Withins, is that of *Wuthering Heights* in Emily Brontë's famous novel. The farm is not the one described by Emily in her book but the setting is. The Brontë siblings would have walked this area and known the many tenant farmers and their families. The ruin at Top Withins is one of several abandoned farmsteads in this area of high barren ground.

Over many years the names and spellings of the farms and fields of these moors have been altered and it must be remembered that the local dialect was hard for those, even in neighbouring villages, to understand. Many people could not read or write and names were often misheard and misspelt. We have followed the direction of the Ordnance Survey's spelling of Withins though you may find various alternatives, e.g. Withens and Wythins.

As with most of the walks, you can start from Haworth centre, where you may have arrived using public transport, or from one of the many car parks around the area. For those who wish to take a shorter route we suggest taking your transport to Back Lane, just passed and to the south-west of Stanbury. This village is just over two kilometres west of Haworth, on the narrow road that continues towards Colne and then to Nelson in Lancashire. After passing through Stanbury village, look out for the left fork where the bus turns around, which is Back Lane. Take this lane and continue for a few hundred metres where the road widens suitably to park here without causing any obstruction to passing farm vehicles. For those leaving from Haworth follow West Lane to the Sun Inn and on to the next fork in the road. Take the middle road past the new cemetery and cross the reservoir to Stanbury and walk through the village to Back Lane.

From Back Lane, Lower Laithe Reservoir sits in the valley to the east. Naturally, along with all the other reservoirs in this area, none of these existed in the Brontë era, though it is a blessing for the sake of public health that they were constructed to provide clean drinking water for the emerging industrial towns.

You can now take one of four options to walk over the moors to Withins Heights and it is always a nice idea to make your journey circular, using a different route for the return journey. Have a look at the map and you will see the different routes, including sections of the long-distance Pennine Way footpath. We would suggest walking in an anti-clockwise direction, which will take you on the slightly higher ground on your outward leg.

We have referred to the walks as number 7 and number 8. Walk 7 commences by continuing along Back Lane in a south-westerly direction. Avoid the various paths to the left (south) and keep heading along this well-maintained track, passing a few stone dwellings. You are now in the area known as Upper Heights and are on the Pennine Way, so expect to meet plenty of other hikers on their long-distance challenge.

The walking is relatively easy and because of the significance of this route, not difficult to follow. The terrain becomes increasingly bleak as you pass several stone dwellings, some just the outline of the building's footprint amongst the heather. As you gain height you pass the remains of Lower Withins and Middle Withins farms, both hardly recognisable from the few remaining stones. As the ground rises steeply you will reach Top Withins.

This is a more complete ruin made safe, and still maintained, by the Yorkshire Water Authority. There are several information panels for the hiker to study. They include old photographs of the dwelling when still occupied as a working farm, complete with diagrams of the original layout and use of each building. The house dates back to the Elizabethan era. Note the deep set stone windows and the amazing views across the landscape.

It is very enjoyable to spend some time as this location and use the seats provided, or sit on the higher ground to survey the carefully preserved ruin. Many photographs and pictures exist of this lovely spot and its original farm, which was still in use until the 1930s. Though as you survey the scene, try to imagine the location in a howling gale, with rain lashing down on the livestock and meagre crops. There are days when the cloud never lifts and the temperature is bitingly cold. The prevailing westerly wind has beaten the solitary trees and bent them over towards the east. This area is the highest land looking east between this farm and the Ural mountains of Russia.

Imagine further that whole families lived and worked on these hills, in almost total isolation in times of bad weather, and had to eke out their difficult livelihood on this windswept area of Yorkshire moorland. It may be a very idyllic scene now, but for thousands of tenant farmers in the early part of the nineteenth century, all over the country, this was their complete life. There were no mechanised farming aids and these fields were dug by hand or ploughed using horses or oxen. Very few crops can grow in this acid soil and the ground would only serve a few sheep and dairy cattle. When you walk around this farmhouse you will see carved into the lintel of a room low on the east wall, the word 'Dairy'. For a fascinating account of this building and of the history of Haworth moor and its farms and inhabitants see *The Real Wuthering Heights – The Story of the Withins Farms* by Steven Wood and Peter Brears (2016).

We know from letters, books and poetry, that all the Brontë children loved the moors but especially Emily. In *Wuthering Heights*, moorland provides the backdrop to the story and its people and their habits are central to its purpose. Much of the book refers to nature and the natural beauty of the area and Emily describes it in all weathers and in all seasons. Her characters, especially Catherine and Heathcliff, are absorbed with the environment and are more at home in its wild terrain than the shelter of the isolated farms. Emily goes further and suggests that the wild moorland is, for her heroine, preferable to a Christian view of Heaven. In one passage, Catherine Earnshaw describes a dream she has had to the servant, Nelly Dean, she says;

'If I were in heaven, Nelly, I should be extremely miserable.'

'Because you are not fit to go there,' I answered. 'All sinners would be miserable in Heaven.'

'But it is not for that. I dreamt, once, that I was there.'....

'I was only going to say that heaven did not seem to be my home; and I broke my heart with weeping to come back to earth; and the angels were so angry that they flung me out, into the middle of the heath on the top of Wuthering Heights; where I woke sobbing for joy.'

Emily Brontë, *Wuthering Heights*

Emily Brontë's love of the moors and her expression of them in her novel, is not to everyone's taste, but she found a solace on the hills and in the valleys and a communion with nature that both challenged and complimented her Christian faith. For Emily, God was found in nature and life and death were all part of the natural cycle that echoed in the moorland surrounding her home and which was, in essence, a part of her home.

In order to supplement their wages many farming families took in cloth to comb or weave or sent their sons to work in the quarries and their daughters to the textile mills. Education was not a priority but learning about husbandry, agriculture and textiles was a major concern. Fuel had to be dug and dried and stockpiled for the winter. The diet for the hill farmers and their families consisted mainly of oatcake, water and broth. Pigs, chickens and geese would help to substitute the diet alongside any wild animals caught or shot on the moors.

The Pennine Way continues to the south-west, on a well maintained paved path to minimise the environmental damage that thousands of heavy walking boots could do to the fragile nature of the thin soil. To the west, (at around 445 metres height), is the area known as Within Heights, after which the ground starts to fall away steeply to Walshaw Dean Upper and Lower Reservoirs.

To return to your start location, leave Top Withins taking the path to the north-east, heading back towards Haworth. This is again a well-defined route, but do check with the map to be sure you are on the correct path. Height will be lost as you walk down towards South Dean Beck. Again, there are options to extend the length of your walk, but we suggest heading almost due east to the path that leads down to the Brontë Bridge and also the Brontë Waterfall. Although Brontë Bridge is not on your intended route, if you have not visited this location before, it is a delightful area and only a short extra distance to add to your walk, (see walk numbers 13 and 14 for further details of two walks in this area).

Returning to the main route, you will be heading more northerly, to ultimately return to Back Lane and your transport. Always a most exhilarating walk and one filled with interest to Brontë enthusiasts. The Brontës often referred to their walks across the moors and as children these lovely hills and valleys must have fired their youthful imaginations. The complete walk is a little over six kilometres, (four miles).

Fact File – Walk 7: Circular walk to Top Withins.

Start/Finish – Grid ref: SE 003 366

OS Maps: OL21 (1:25,000), Landranger 103 (1:50,000)

Start/finish: Back Lane, off Main Street, Stanbury, 2km west of Haworth.

General Information – a few steep hills and exposed moorland paths, 5-6km, allow over 2-3 hours, (we recommend you check the weather forecast before you commence walking over the moors).

Stanbury village has inns along Main Street or 2km to Haworth. Roadside parking, but please do not create an obstruction to large agricultural vehicles.

Walk 8

Walk number 8 is of similar length to Walk 7, but enables another circular trek with the prize of Top Withins in the middle of your route. It is a more northerly route taking you passed Stanbury Moor and Withins Slack.

Take the road that leaves Back Lane in a westerly direction. Walk a little under a kilometre passed Cold Knowle End Farm to your right and on to Buckley Green. Here you need to fork left and pass the house of one of the last traditional weavers in the north of England, Timothy Feather, (1825–1910) As stated, his unique status and importance to the history of home weavers has been recognised, with his original loom, along with a very 'life-like' wax figure of the man himself, now housed in the Cliff Castle Museum to the north of Keighley town centre,

Continuing along what is now a path, head for Far Slack Farm on your right, where you take the left path (south). Climbing steadily, you take the right-hand path (west) after only a few hundred metres and then continue west-south-west over Stanbury Moor, before sweeping around to approach the ruin of Top Withins from the north side. As with the last walk, spend some time here reading the information boards and drinking in the splendid views from this isolated location.

The return route is away to the north east, (though not following the Pennine Way). Lose height down to South Dean Beck, but this time, take a left fork staying on slightly higher ground to Walk 7. This more direct route north-west will return you to Back Lane and your start point. An excellent walk of around six kilometres, (four miles) taking up to two hours or including however long you wish to enjoy the area around Top Withins.

These two walks take you into some of the loveliest and loneliest countryside for many miles and is such a contrast to the noise and bustle of the towns and cities. Spending time watching the birds and listening to their sounds is a joy. Smelling the fresh air and the heather is so different and clean from the pollution we are all subject to. Watching the sky constantly changing and enjoying the exhilaration of the prospect is a wonderful experience. Whatever the weather or the season many people love this spot and have written about it for centuries. Emily Brontë, whilst living and working away from her beloved Parsonage home and the surrounding moors, sat daydreaming one day during a brief rest from her duties. As she remembered the places she loved she wrote the following verses which are from her poem, Stanzas.

> *There is a spot mid barren hills*
> *Where winter howls and driving rain,*
> *But if the dreary tempest chills*
> *There is a light that warms again.*
>
> *The house is old, the trees are bare*
> *And moonless bends the misty dome*
> *But what on earth is half as dear,*
> *So longed for as the hearth of home?*
>
> *The mute bird sitting on the stone,*
> *The dank moss dripping from the wall,*
> *The garden-walk the weeds o'er-grown,*
> *I love them – how I love them all!*
>
> *Shall I go there? Or shall I seek*
> *Another clime, another sky,*

Where tongues familiar music speak
In accents dear to memory?

Yes, as I mused, the naked room,
The flickering firelight died away
And from the midst of cheerless gloom
I passed to bright, unclouded day –

A little and a lone green lane,
That opened on a common wide;
A distant, dreamy, dim blue chain
Of mountains circling every side;

A heaven so clear, an earth so calm,
So sweet, so soft, so hushed an air
And, deepening still the dream-like charm
Wild moor-sheep feeding everywhere –

That was the scene; I knew it well,
I knew the path-ways far and near
That winding o'er each billowy swell
Marked out the tracks of wandering deer.

Could I have lingered but an hour
It well had paid a week of toil,
But truth has banished fancy's power;
I hear my dungeon bars recoil –

Even as I stood with raptured eye
Absorbed in bliss so deep and dear
My hour of rest had fleeted by
And given me back to weary care

Emily Brontë. *December 1838*

When you are wandering around these moors you are walking in the footsteps of Emily Brontë and visiting the sites that she and her sisters loved.

Take your time and relish these special places and appreciate the sights and sounds that others before you have treasured so much. Whilst enjoying this place here and now remember that in the future people will follow you. If we are to keep these open and beautiful moorlands we must all be careful to leave no evidence that could upset or spoil its endless charm for future generations.

Fact File – Walk 8: Circular walk to Buckley Green and Top Withins.

Start/Finish – Grid ref: SE 003 367

OS Maps: OL21 (1:25,000), Landranger 103 (1:50,000)

Start/finish: Back Lane, off Main Street, Stanbury, 2km west of Haworth.

General Information – a few steep hills and exposed moorland paths, 5-6km, allow over 2-3 hours, (we recommend you check the weather forecast before you commence walking over the moors).

Stanbury village has two inns along Main Street, or just 2km to Haworth. Roadside parking, but please do not create an obstruction to large agricultural vehicles.

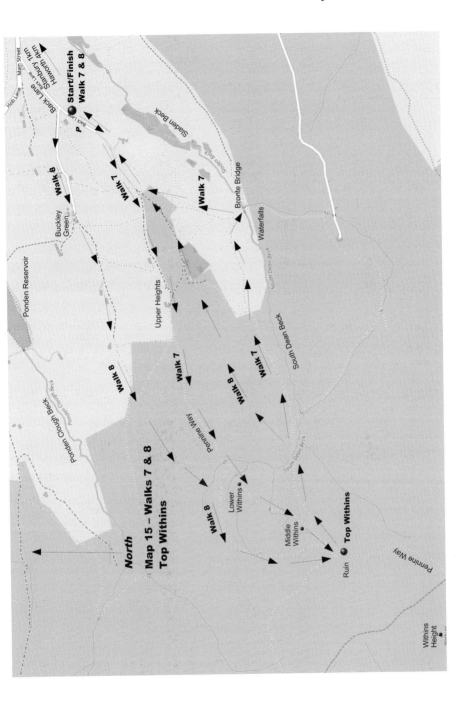

Map 15 – Walks 7 & 8
Top Withins

North

Start/Finish
Walk 7 & 8

Walk 8

Walk 7

Walk 7

Buckley Green

Ponden Reservoir

Ponden Clough Beck

Walk 8

Walk 7

Walk 8

Walk 7

Walk 7

Upper Heights

Pennine Way

Walk 8

Lower Withins

Middle Withins

Top Withins

Ruin

Withins Height

Bronte Bridge

Waterfalls

Sladen Beck

Sladen Beck

South Dean Beck

South Dean Beck

South Dean Beck

Pennine Way

Haworth 4km

Stanbury 1km

Main Street

High Lane

Back Lane

Back Lane

King Street

Above: Striding out along Back Lane towards Top Withins, with Lower Laithe Reservoir and Stanbury in the distance.

Below: As you gain height walking towards Withins Heights, the views looking back over the moors towards Haworth are magnificent. South Dean Beck cuts its path east under the Bronte Bridge and continues to flow as Sladen Beck to Lower Laithe Reservoir.

Above: Now looking back from Withins Heights to the ruin of Top Withins Farm. The remoteness of this location and the hardship the farmers had to face to eke out a living on these bleak moors, is so apparent.

Below: Look out for this stone plaque on the ruins of Top Withins, commemorating the association with Emily's '*Wuthering Heights*' novel. She would regularly walk to this location, both with her brother and sisters, and with her beloved dogs as she grew older.

Above: View through one of the stone windows in the south wall of Top Withins Farm, looking out across Withins Heights.

Below: Looking to the north east at the ruin of Top Withins with one of the many boundary stones in the foreground. These substantial stones were used to mark boundaries, land ownership or way markers across the moors and would often have initials engraved or the number of miles to the next location.

Above: An interesting view looking south over Top Withins, which gives you a good idea of the size and footprint of the farm buildings.

Below: Heading east, this is where you take the path to your right that takes a line parallel to South Dean Beck and along to Brontë Bridge just over a kilometre away.

Above: The path makes a steep decent down to Brontë Bridge, with Brontë Falls hidden by the undergrowth in the gulley opposite.

Below: This tranquil view is looking west, with South Dean Beck flowing under the Brontë Bridge. A stone plaque commemorates the re-building of this structure after one of the many flash floods created by sudden heavy storms over the moors above.

Chapter 13

Ponden Hall, Ponden Kirk and Buckley Green

Walks 9 and 10

At two kilometres due west of Stanbury, Ponden Hall stands to the south-west side of Ponden Reservoir. A wonderful setting that in some ways has been enhanced by the positioning of the 'modern' reservoir. Our two walks are quite short in distance, with both at around three kilometres long (two miles), but they are filled with splendid views as we take a circular route to Ponden Kirk to the west-south-west, and a pleasant walk south to Buckley Green.

As with Walks 7 and 8, you commence your travels by leaving Haworth to the west, taking West Lane and Sun Lane. A little way before you reach Stanbury, on the right-hand side of the road is a cemetery built by the Oakworth Local Board in 1888. It had a small chapel, now demolished, and contains interesting war memorials. Like all the cemeteries in this area it is worth a peaceful walk amongst the gravestones to view the names and lives of the local population. Before the creation of this cemetery, Stanbury people were carried to Haworth, often in long processions with mourners singing as they went.

Stanbury is an attractive moorland village, set high on a ridge overlooking Haworth Moor and the valley of Sladen Beck and Ponden Reservoir and has existed here for centuries. There are some beautiful buildings and it has a long history of notable people and events. As you enter the village from the east you will see the '*Manor*' house on your right. This was the home of the Taylor family; landowners and also trustees of Haworth Church and friends of Patrick Brontë. There is no manor of Stanbury as it is a part of the Manor of Bradford and is in the Parish of Haworth. The village had three public houses but now has two, The Friendly Inn and The Wuthering Heights. Both hostelries provide excellent food and the Friendly Inn also offers accommodation.

During the 1840s the main occupation of the then nearly 1,000 inhabitants of Stanbury, was handloom weaving and wool-combing. The farms were all occupied and many people rented fields for crop growing; mainly potatoes, oats and barley. Family names in the village included many Sunderlands, Ratcliffes, Heys, Taylors, Midgleys, Heatons and Shackletons. The village boasted a school, built in 1805 and this was superseded by the Board School of 1882 which still stands a little way back from the road, on the left before you leave the village. The school had various schoolmasters but none so famous as Jonas Bradley, a remarkable man and a gifted teacher who arrived in 1889. He taught in a very new and interesting style that saw him taking the children out into the fields and lanes to learn about and appreciate natural history. His forward thinking and innovative teaching style were recognised and respected in the neighbourhood for many years.

The school stands opposite a small green enclosed plot of land that is the former Quaker burial ground, note the cross in the dry stone wall at the roadside. The villagers all attended various churches and chapels in the nineteenth century. They had the choice of the small St Gabriel's Church on your right as you walk through the village. This was built in 1848 with the assistance and drive of the Rev. Arthur Bell Nicholls who helped to raise public subscriptions. It contains the top of the Grimshaw and Brontës' three-decker pulpit from Haworth old church. A Wesleyan chapel, now converted into houses, was built in 1832 and closed in 1966. There was a further undenominational chapel/place of worship at Scar Top. It was first founded as a Sunday School, in 1818, and then a Chapel was erected in 1869 which incorporated people of various religious beliefs. It is actually just outside the Haworth parish area. Scar Top chapel was hugely popular and held events to which thousands of people attended. It's annual 'Charity' event became so large that if the weather was fine it was held on land at Ponden Corn Mill to accommodate everyone in the open air. There was a large band of musicians and an equally large choir. Races and a tea were held as well as two services by preachers with the ability to hold outdoor services, in the Evangelical fashion. There is a lovely description of a 'Charity' held in Scar Top Church, in Joseph Craven's book on Stanbury. He writes that,

If anyone had gone into Stanbury on 'Charity Day,' no matter how early, he might have seen every one on the move and ready to entertain all and sundry. Open houses were common. By eight or nine o'clock in the morning men would be seen coming into the village with their fiddle boxes under their arms. About ten o'clock you would see the people flocking to the Chapel to hear the singers and players practice for the afternoon and evening service…. (The Choir) would see trebles in the centre, above them the altos, on one side the tenors, and on the other the basses…On the back you would see and hear the fiddles, first and second, and the viola or tenor fiddle, and the little bass fiddle; sometimes the big bass fiddle and the flute would have a place, the cornet, the trombone, and, on one occasion, the ophicleide.

Joseph Craven, *A Brontë Moorland Village and its People: A History of Stanbury* 1907

These church events were a wonderful entertainment for people who had very little time or capacity for amusement and fun. The annual charity days were often a place for young couples to meet and a generally good time was had by everyone working in harmony and enjoying each other's company. They often included long processions of people walking through the lanes and villages singing hymns and anthems. You can see Scar Top chapel today at the junction of the lane that crosses Ponden Reservoir and the road to Colne.

A little further on and to the west of Stanbury, at a place known as Silver Hill, is a large mound of unknown origin. Now surrounded by a drystone wall it was probably a natural phenomenon caused by glaciation but may have been used as a look out on to the old Turnpike Road.

The Brontës were visitors to Stanbury on many occasions and would almost certainly have made the journey on foot from the Parsonage, 2 kilometres due east. At that time, before the building of the reservoir, (1920s), they would often walk into the valley and climb up the hillside to Stanbury where they may have called on the Taylor family or made various visits on behalf of their father. Charlotte would probably have assisted her husband at St Gabriel's Church. See also Map 4 for Stanbury village.

Continue through the village on what is now Hob Lane, pass Back Lane and then you need to look out for a left turn after one kilometre. This is the narrow Ponden Lane which passes by the original Ponden Mill, tight up to the road on your right-hand side. This former mill has recently been restored and opened for Bed and Breakfast and houses a café and a parking area in its charming location beside the Ponden Clough Beck, which runs into the river Worth.

Keep following Ponden Lane for a further kilometre, with the reservoir to your right and a sharp right-hand bend at the head of the water. Park with consideration to others in this area. The road has been widened, so you should not be creating an obstruction here. Again, we will describe the route in an anti-clockwise direction, taking the high ground first.

Walk 9

For this walk, head north along Ponden Lane the short distance to the historic Ponden Hall at the right-hand side of the lane and Ponden Guest House to the left. Both these buildings are of historic significance and have been lovingly restored by their current owners.

Both offer Bed and Breakfast and a marvellous range of meals for residents and walkers. Typical of the design of country houses in these parts, they look magnificent in this setting.

These houses and outbuildings are the original seat of the Heaton family, who owned many acres of land in the district and built and ran Ponden Mill, owned stone quarries and were gentleman farmers. Many generations of Heaton's lived and worked here and they were trustees of Haworth church lands as early as 1559. They were also jurymen and constables and were involved especially with the small, original Scar Top chapel. An avenue of trees once ran from Ponden Hall through the valley to the chapel, all now lost beneath the waters of Ponden Reservoir. The Heaton's of the time were well known to the Brontë family. Tracing Heaton history is a little difficult as alternate generations named their eldest sons, Robert or Michael.

The building to your left, Ponden House, was either the original house or another Heaton dwelling and was a ruin until its restoration by the current owner, Brenda Taylor. Brenda formerly lived at Ponden Hall where, as now, she welcomed hundreds of walkers and holidaymakers. The large Hall opposite probably dates back to the sixteenth century and possibly earlier. It was extended in 1801, as described on the engraved stone above the doorway to the left of the main hall building.

The Heaton family were wealthy and followed all the pursuits of the country gentry. They kept a pack of hounds for hunting and their retainers and servants often stayed with the family for generations doing the same work. John Bolton was one of a long family of huntsmen who looked after the horses and hounds.

Interestingly, *Wuthering Heights* begins with a description of the stone over the doorway of the Heights, also stating the date of 1801. Whilst Ponden Hall has little bearing on the Heights of Emily's novel, she may well have used this more sheltered location and the wealth and standing of the Heaton's, when describing the Linton family in her novel and their home, Thrushcross Grange, in the valley below Wuthering Heights farm.

The current owners of both Ponden Hall and Ponden House, offer superb hotel facilities and events and have restored the fabric of their houses and modernised them in such a tasteful way as to offer all the atmosphere of its original rooms and location with all the comforts of modern living.

The affluent Heaton's held a superb collection of books at Ponden Hall and the Brontë siblings and their father may have borrowed volumes from this library. It is said to have included a first folio of Shakespeare's plays. Unfortunately, following the death of the last Heaton occupants in 1898, the contents of the library were sold and dispersed.

The history of the Heaton's is inextricably linked with Haworth and there are many documents tracing the lives and times of various members of the family and their effect on the town and its people. One item that may link Ponden Hall and the novel, *Wuthering Heights* is the description in the book of an enormous Tudor, carved, oak dresser; a similar one of which was housed in Ponden Hall for generations and would have been seen by Emily. It is now on display at East Riddlesden Hall, near Keighley; a beautiful National Trust property open to the public.

Continue west along Ponden Lane for a few hundred metres before turning left, (south) and following this narrow lane as it swings round to the west. It is around 500 metres to where you approach a crossroad of tracks and you want to head left (south) towards Ponden Slack.

Head along the wall as you gain height up to Bracken Hill. The steep escarpment to your left falls away to Ponden Clough Beck and ahead is Ponden Kirk, You approach by keeping to the high ground, taking a longer route around the contours, then turning back on yourself.

Ponden Kirk is another beautiful place amongst these wild moorlands. It is mentioned in *Wuthering Heights* as the trysting place where the ghosts of Cathy and Heathcliff are seen. This lovely stone cliff with its deep set holes and clefts is thought to have been associated, centuries ago, with the Druids. Local legend states that if a maiden crawls through the narrow space in the rock she will be married within the year. This is not an invitation to try and when you are near this area be very careful indeed. The sides of the cliffs are steep and slippery and even the path above can be fairly treacherous, especially in bad weather. It is not a suitable place for children to wander without strict supervision.

The water gushes down the escarpment at Ponden Kirk and at this wonderful setting, you can cross over the stream for a slightly longer return walk, (marked as walk 10 on the map), keeping to the higher ground passed Birch Brink, or follow the steep series of steps down by the side of the beck, (walk 9). These steps can become very slippery and many are uneven. A hand rail is provided but do take particular care in wet weather. You cross the stream at the bottom and follow the track running parallel to the path you have come along, but at a lower level. Eventually this path re-joins the one you took from Ponden Hall, to complete your route back to the starting point.

The walk packs a great deal into a short length, combining historical locations, a few climbs, excellent views and the delightful waters of Ponden Clough Beck. Allow a few hours, as parts of it are steep and are exposed in inclement weather. You may wish to remain in the area to take in the next circular walk to Buckley Green (walk 10) and the same location close to Ponden Reservoir can be used as your start and finish point.

Fact File – Walk 9: Ponden Hall, Ponden Slack and Ponden Kirk.

Start/Finish – Grid ref: SD 992 369

OS Maps: OL21 (1:25,000), Landranger 103 (1:50,000)

Start/finish: Ponden Lane, Ponden Reservoir, 2km west of Stanbury, 4km west of Haworth.

General Information – a few steep hills and exposed moorland paths, 5km, allow over 2-3 hours.

2km east to Stanbury village, inns along Main Street. Plenty of locations to park, but please be clear of gateways and away from agricultural machinery.

Walk 10

The alternative route over Birch Brink takes a more southerly route, before a steady descent back down to the beck and approaching Ponden Hall from the south.

The first section of walk 10 follows the same route as walk 9 from Ponden Reservoir, passed the Hall and the high ground around Bracken Hill to Ponden Kirk. At this stream the water rushes down to form Ponden Clough Beck flowing easterly to the reservoir. Where the steep steps taken for walk 9 drop down the side of the waterfalls, walk 10 crosses over the footbridge at this location.

Walking almost due east, we follow the contours around the southern side of this valley and walk over Birch Brink. The path is generally easy to follow, even when ferns and heather are high in the summer, with occasional maker posts to further guide you. Looking to your left, (north), there is a splendid view across the valley where you can see your route and that of walk 9, at a lower level on the far slopes.

Around 1km east of the footbridge, you have an option to head north east, down the slope towards Lower Slack farm and the reservoir beyond. Keeping to the higher ground, continue walking east to Far Slack, which you pass on the south side. You are now walking on a track which soon passes Near Slack, still heading easterly to Buckley Green. This charming hamlet includes the former cottage of Timothy Feather, the last handloom weaver.

Several paths and tracks join the route around Buckley Green, but you want to be heading due north here, again on a well-defined track, as it also forms part of the Pennine Way. It is a little under 500 metres to Rush Isles and then Ponden Lane running east-west. Turn left, (west) and walk along the lane with the reservoir to your right and back to your starting point close to Ponden Hall.

The area is criss-crossed with footpaths and has three of the long distance paths in the vicinity: the Pennine Way, the Brontë Way and the Millennium Way. Plenty of specialist guides have been produced to cover these long-distance walks in greater detail. It is important to give credit to the individuals and organisations who have worked tirelessly and over many years to establish these significant tracks for generations of walkers to enjoy. They each form a wonderful opportunity for walkers and tourists alike, to enjoy uninterrupted access to the countryside on easy to follow routes, complete with their guides to the area.

On the adjoining map, we have highlighted the many locations you can enjoy in a circular walk, taking in Buckley Green, Upper Heights and Lower Slacks. We guide you along one of the options (walk 10), but you can increase your walk by taking any of the others.

This is a good area to test your skills at creating your own circular walk from the location at Ponden Reservoir. Have a good look at the large scale Ordnance Survey map of this area and you will quickly see that many alternatives can be taken. Short circular walks like this one, are ideal for sharpening up your map reading skills: lots of short options with many clues to follow your route from farm to farm, or along a river valley. You are never far from your starting point and it is also handy if you need to head home due to changes in the weather.

Fact File – Walk 10: Ponden Hall, Ponden Kirk to Buckley Green, Circular.

Start/Finish – Grid ref: SD 994 370

OS Maps: OL21 (1:25,000), Landranger 103 (1:50,000)

Start/finish: Ponden Lane, Ponden Reservoir, 2km west of Stanbury, 4km west of Haworth.

General Information – some steep hills and uneven and exposed moorland paths around the top of the valley and especially above the kirk and the path leading back down to the bridge over Ponden Clough Beck. Extra care needed throughout the year but especially in bad weather. 5km, allow up to 3 hours.

Many opportunities to make short circular walks around Buckley Green, Upper Heights and down to Lower Slack. Some paths can be overgrown in summer, so have your OS maps to hand.

Stanbury village has inns along Main Street or 2km to Haworth.

Plenty of parking opportunities, please be clear of gateways and ensure your vehicle is well positioned. Note that Stanbury village has a speed restriction of 20mph and is served by a primary school on the south side of the road towards the west end of the village.

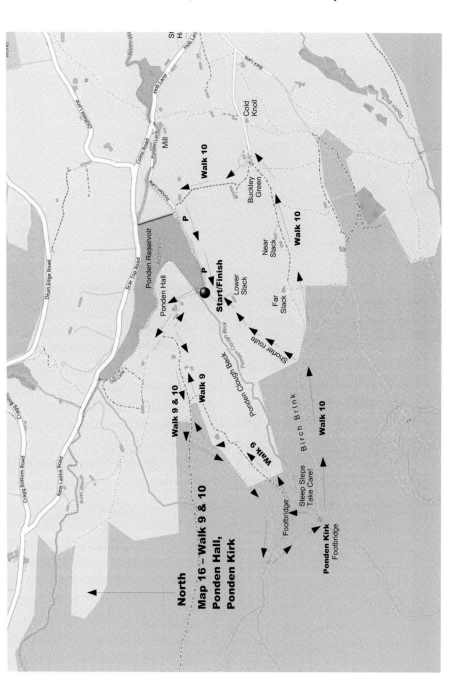

Built in 1848,
at the instigation
and aid of
the Rev Arthur
Bell Nicholls,
Charlotte
Brontë's
husband,
St Gabriel's
Church stands at
the north side of
the road through
Stanbury village.

Above left: The top section of the Grimshaw and Brontë three-decker pulpit, which originally adorned Haworth Church. Thousands of sermons were delivered from this pulpit by these two men and many others, including the Wesley brothers. It originally had a sounding board positioned above it to help to project the preacher's voice to the congregations at Haworth. Inside the small church of St Gabriel's such a facility is not necessary.

Above right: This fascinating stone cross built into the dry stone wall around the former Quaker burial ground in Stanbury.

First built as an undenominational
Sunday school in 1818, Scar Top Chapel
dates from 1869 and is adjacent to the
road, 2km west of Stanbury village, next
to Ponden Reservoir.

'The Friendly'
public house is
located on the
north side of the
narrow road through
Stanbury village.

The 'Wuthering
Heights Inn' is a
little further along
the road towards
Haworth. Both inns
contain beautiful
period bars with
memorabilia from
the past.

Above: This plaque commemorates the rebuilding of Ponden House, opposite Ponden Hall, on the south side of the lane.

Below: The sheltered courtyard entrance to Ponden Hall is to the right of the narrow lane as you walk away from the reservoir.

Above: This stone tablet over the entrance to Ponden Hall commemorates the original building of the Hall by the Heaton family in 1680 and the alterations and extensions of 1801. The Brontës were visitors to the Heaton's and may have had access to their extensive library.

Below: Around 600m west of Ponden Hall, this is the location where you take the left path and head south. A look at the track ahead, (west), gives you a good guide of a trek over to Lancashire two centuries ago. Now imagine the track in low cloud, a cold wind and constant rain: a daunting prospect for the travellers before the age of the railways.

Above: It is only a short distance before this way marker confirms the locations to turn right, south- west, on the high route to Ponden Kirk.

Below: Cross carefully over the stream as it flows over the rocks and change your direction towards Ponden Kirk. The views over the valley below are wonderful.

Above: The outcrops of rocks form a wonderful setting, but be sure to keep away from the long drop below. You can see the path (walk number 9), at the lower level beneath you.

Below: A long way down, but tempting for children to squeeze through!

Above: The small wooden bridge over Ponden Clough Beck, with the path leading back to the higher ground, (walk number 10). To the east and avoiding the crossing, the path, (walk number 9), descends the steep, slippery steps alongside the beck. You return by walking around the valley at a lower level and back towards Ponden Hall.

Below: Looking up towards the wooden bridge, notice how uneven the steps are, so despite the handrail, take great care especially when wet.

Above: Another view looking down the steep steps, with the weir to the side, as the beck descends to Ponden Clough.

Below: Looking back at the route of walk 9 to the weir, with the steps up to the wooden bridge over Ponden Clough Beck. The route you have covered is along the top of the escarpment and you can see the high rocks at the top right of the picture. Walk 10 is to the high ground at the top left.

Above: Walk 10 over Birch Brink, with the ground falling away to the left, (north), down to Ponden Clough and the reservoir in the distance. You have the option at this location, to fork left and descend down to Lower Slack and Ponden Reservoir beyond. The path straight on takes you on the longer route towards Far Slack and Buckley Green.

Below: In the height of summer, ferns grow waist high, but the path can still be followed with occasional way markers confirming your route.

Above: Looking back over Walk 10, you can follow the route you have covered around the head of the valley, with Walk 9 at the lower level to the right and Ponden Clough Beck flowing easterly.

Below: This attractive sign confirms that you are at Buckley Green.

Chapter 14

Wycoller Hall and Country Park

Walks 11 and 12

Unless you are walking the full length of the Brontë Way, you will need transport from Haworth to reach your next location with connections to the Brontë sisters. Wycoller Hall and the surrounding Country Park are around ten kilometres (six miles) west of Haworth. This delightful Hall and setting is one that people suggest for the location of Ferndean Manor, in *Jane Eyre*. Complete with a romantic ruin, set in beautiful woodland surroundings, along with a succession of unique bridges over Wycoller Beck, it is a delightful secret spot that many tourists often miss.

It is likely that the Brontë children will have visited this place, probably many times. The Hall was originally built by Piers Hartley in the 1500s and passed by marriage to the Cunliffe family in 1611. This family lost their ancestral home through debts and moved permanently into Wycoller in 1720. However, for much of its life, Wycoller Hall was unoccupied except in the shooting season. In the early 1800s the Hall was held by Charles Cunliffe-Owen, but he too had many debts and sold off various parts of the estate. Throughout much of the nineteenth century the Hall was unoccupied and gradually fell in to ruin. Lancashire County Council bought the hamlet and estate from the Water Board in 1973 and Wycoller was declared a conservation area and the surrounding 350 acres, a Country Park.

In *Jane Eyre*, Charlotte Brontë describes Jane searching for Ferndean House and Mr Rochester and wandering through the woods in the twilight. She wrote,

The manor-house of Ferndean was a building of considerable antiquity, moderate size, and no architectural pretensions, deep buried in a wood. I had heard of it before. Mr Rochester often spoke of it, and sometimes went there. His father had purchased the estate for the sake of the game covers. He would have let the house but could find no tenant, in consequence of its ineligible and insalubrious site. Ferndean then remained uninhabited and unfurnished.... I proceeded: at last my way opened, the trees thinned a little; presently I beheld a railing, then the house – scarce, by this dim light, distinguishable from the trees; so dank and green were its decaying walls. Entering a portal, fastened only by a latch, I stood amidst a space of enclosed ground, from which the wood swept away in a semi-circle.... The house presented two pointed gables in its front; the windows were latticed and narrow; the front door was narrow too, one step led up to it.... It was as still as a church on a weekday: the pattering rain on the forest leaves was the only sound audible in its vicinage.

Charlotte Brontë, *Jane Eyre.*

The walk can be a slow amble from a car park around one kilometre to the west of Wycoller Hall (walk 11), or from a car park and viewpoint just off the road between Haworth and Colne (Two Laws Road) north-east of the ruin (walk 12). Like so many of the walks in this book, you then have many options to make a circular trek of a few hours, or just a relaxing meander around the ruins and over the ancient old bridges that cross over the beck. There is also a pleasant café in the small hamlet of Wycoller, with a gift and sweet shop.

Walk 11

This first option is to walk from the car park to the west of Wycoller. This is around 2 kilometres west of Trawdon, along a narrow country lane. A small charge is made at this car park but please do not proceed into the hamlet in your vehicle unless you are disabled. All the lanes are very narrow and you will be obstructing the handful of residents who live in this delightful place.

Leave the car park and head east along the well maintained path, running parallel to the lane. Follow this path alongside the narrow road, through to the hamlet. If it is dry, you can also take a field path on your right that takes you to your destination.

As you near Wycoller Beck, your first sight of the ruin of Wycoller Hall and some of the old bridges come into view. The first of these bridges has been built as a twin stone arch bridge, just wide enough for a person with a horse to cross. The stones are heavily worn with the centuries of feet and hooves, taking their toll on the hard surfaces. The arches themselves have a remarkable distortion, yet still carry their load after so many years.

Once over this first bridge, continue the short distance to the ruins. They beckon you to explore from room to room, as you try to envisage the once splendour of this gentleman's country lodge. Some information panels guide you around the ruins and on to an interesting display in the Cruck Barn Archaeological Museum to the east of the former house. Here you can learn more about the area and its fascinating history. There are also public toilets and a picnic area just behind this building, and a large pond beyond. This really is a beautiful location to meander through the trees, along the banks of the beck, crossing over the bridges or just sitting by the ruins of the old Hall. You can permit your mind to wander, as the Brontë's most certainly did, and you can well imagine how it would appeal to writers of romantic and historic fiction.

After your walk south-east, along the beck, you can head back to your transport at the Wycoller Country Park car park, with a stroll back through the hamlet, or by using the field path (see the map). Whichever of these shorter routes you choose, this will have been a very relaxing walk in an amazing setting.

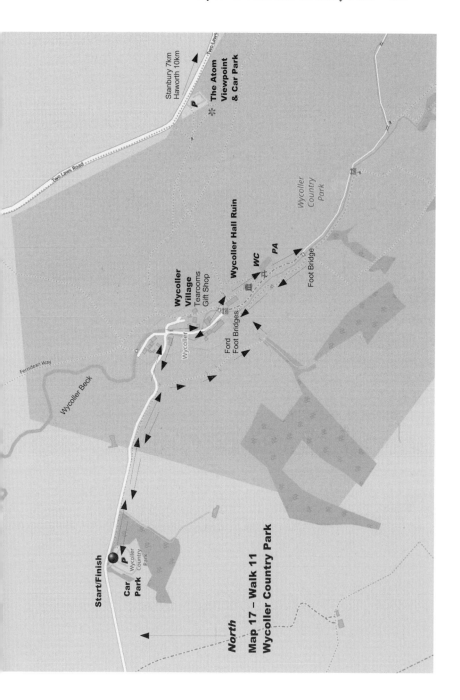

Stanbury 7km
Haworth 10km

Two Laws

**The Atom
Viewpoint
& Car Park**

P

Two Laws Road

Wycoller Beck

Ferndean Way

**Wycoller
Village**
Tearooms
Gift Shop

Wycoller

Wycoller Hall Ruin

WC

PA

Wycoller
Country
Park

Ford
Foot Bridges

Foot Bridge

Wycoller Beck

Start/Finish

**Car
Park**

P

Wycoller
Country
Park

North

**Map 17 – Walk 11
Wycoller Country Park**

Above: Walking easterly towards the hamlet of Wycoller, you can follow the narrow lane, but you do have the option to take the field path down to the ruins of Wycoller Hall.

Below: Can there be a more romantic setting with the ruins of Wycoller Hall beyond the wonderful double arch, stone packhorse bridge across Wycoller Beck?

Above: The ruins of Wycoller Hall.

Below: This substantial fireplace once adorned one of the many rooms inside the Hall, but now forms a nice seating area for walkers. There is a large barn and information centre also nearby. This building is manned by volunteers and is worth a visit. It contains lots of interesting artefacts and a beautiful wooden beamed roof.

Looking north through the ruins of Wycoller Hall.

The meadow and ponds to the south of Wycoller Hall with picnic tables and toilet facilities.

The picturesque setting of the ford across Wycoller Beck which lies between the two stone bridges with the ruin of Wycoller Hall in the background.

Above: Another view of the double stone arch bridge over Wycoller Beck, with the extraordinary distortion to the left arch of the centuries old structure.

Below: A unique stone slab bridge just upstream of the ford and stone arch bridge.

Fact File – Walk 11: Wycoller Hall and Country Park.

Start/Finish – Grid ref: SD 926 394

OS Maps: OL21 (1:25,000), Landranger 103 (1:50,000)

Start/finish: Car Park clearly signed 1km west of Wycoller village, (small charge for cars), 2km west of Trawden. Take the Colne road west from Haworth, turn left just before Laneshaw Bridge. This road route from Haworth to Wycoller is approximately 15 kilometres (10 miles). Please do not park in the very narrow lanes of the hamlet of Wycoller.

General Information – mostly level paths, some grass walking, 4km, allow 1-2 hours.

Public toilets in Country Park, Visitor Centre in the Aisled Museum Barn behind the ruin, delightful craft centre and tea room in Wycoller.

Walk 12

For a longer walk, you will see that we have highlighted several circular routes, which are easy to follow and take in more of Wycoller Country Park to the south-east and along the beck. Another approach is to start and finish your walk from the car park at the higher level, to the east of Wycoller Hall. Walk 12 is accessed off Two Laws Road and is an excellent viewpoint across the valley.

The road from Haworth up here and beyond into Lancashire, is the one that the four eldest Brontë girls would all have taken when their father took them to the Clergy Daughters' School, at Cowan Bridge. This is the school described as 'Lowood' in *Jane Eyre*. It was the school from which Maria and Elizabeth returned home gravely ill and died soon afterwards, aged only 11 and 10 years respectively. It is where the tuberculosis virus was possibly first introduced into the Brontë family and eventually caused the deaths of each of the six siblings.

Leave your vehicle in the car parking area beside the road where there is a sign for The Atom Car Park and see the modern art sculpture, 'The Atom' as the prominent landmark. You can decide whether this structure enhances the landscape or not, but it certainly offers a superb viewing point but it certainly offers a superb viewing point looking out over the surrounding countryside. As part of the Panopticon Project for Pendle, it was designed by Peter Meacock in the early years of this millennium. Its unusual igloo shape can be used as a shelter, should the Pennine rain be falling around you, and its round fenestral openings offer a unique view of the surrounding valley and countryside.

You are less than a kilometre from Wycoller Hall, walking south west across the fields, but we suggest that you set off to the east and make a circular walk of around six kilometres and take in part of the Brontë Way, with several kilometres hugging the banks of Wycoller Beck.

Keeping to the higher ground, head towards Foster's Leap Farm, where the path swings around to the south-east and on to Smithy's Clough and Parson Lee Farm. Here, you cross over the beck for the first of many times and head west along the narrow lane. You can cross the beck on several bridges, some following our route, other times just to be drawn over the beck as you wish to sample the quaint setting of many of the bridges. One particular footbridge is constructed by the placing of a very heavy single stone slab, at an angle from one bank to the other. It has clearly dominated this location for many years, yet you stare in wonder as to how it remains in situ with its ends seemingly to barely touch the beck sides. Do walk across, even though you need to cross back onto the track, as you follow the stream towards Wycoller.

As you will see from the map, you can approach the ruins from either side of the beck, as you near the small hamlet. As with the first walk, meander along through these stone ruins; this is not a walk to be hurried. Soak up the atmosphere of the area whilst looking forward to a pot of tea in the café or enjoy a picnic beside the waters. Some of our Brontë locations are wild, barren places, but not this one. It is a purely romantic setting; as if a pre-Raphaelite artist were trying to incorporate as many beautiful and natural features as possible onto one canvas. The result is stunning as Wycoller incorporates a medieval atmosphere with the nostalgia of history in an Elysian setting.

To return to 'The Atom' and the car park you have two possible routes, both with a short but steep climb, back up to the viewpoint and the splendid panorama over the valley. Whichever of the routes you have taken, a most enjoyable stroll to take in another generous portion of Brontë literary history.

Fact File – Walk 12: The Atom, Wycoller Hall and Country Park Circular.

Start/Finish – Grid ref: SD 937 393

OS Maps: OL21 (1:25,000), Landranger 103 (1:50,000)

Start/finish: 'The Atom' car park, clearly signed on the Colne road, 10km west of Haworth.

A few steep hills and exposed paths, 5-6km, allow over 2-3 hours.

General Information – public toilets in Country Park, Visitor Centre in Barn behind Wycoller Hall ruin, delightful craft centre, sweet shop and tearoom, with toilet, in Wycoller Hamlet.

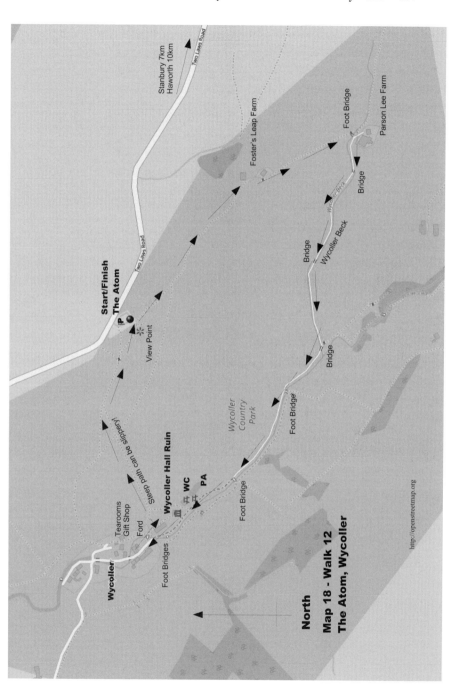

Stanbury 7km
Haworth 10km

Two Laws Road

Foster's Leap Farm

Foot Bridge

Parson Lee Farm

Bridge

Wycoller Beck

Wycoller Brk

Bridge

Start/Finish
The Atom

Two Laws Road

View Point

Bridge

Bridge

Steep path can be slippery!

Wycoller
Country
Park

Foot Bridge

Wycoller Hall Ruin

WC
PA

Foot Bridge

Tearooms
Gift Shop

Ford

Foot Bridge

Wycoller

Foot Bridges

http://openstreetmap.org

North

Map 18 - Walk 12
The Atom, Wycoller

Above: The Atom located high above Wycoller Beck. This viewpoint has two car parks and a picnic area, just south of the road between Haworth and Colne. It is the location for the start/finish of walk 12.

Below: It is a matter of personal taste if you like the modern art of 'The Atom' in this location. Interesting views over the countryside around Wycoller and the Forest of Trawden.

Above: One of the many foot bridges over the beck that take you to the south side and the route of several long distances footpaths. This one is close to Parson Lee Farm.

Below: Follow the signs to Wycoller, with many long distance footpaths taking a route through this wonderful valley.

Above: The waters tumble downstream to form Wycoller Beck.

Below: Just one of the many wonderful aspects of nature to pass on your walk through Wycoller Country Park.

Above: An extraordinary single slab stone bridge over the beck, you just have to walk over it twice to believe it does not collapse under you!

Below: What keeps this slab in place: magic?

Above: Imagine how many horses' hooves and heavy boots it has taken to create such wear to the stone decking of this beautiful bridge.

Below: When you have soaked up all the atmosphere of Wycoller ruins and the beck, head up these steps and back towards the car park at The Atom.

Chapter 15

Brontë Bridge and waterfall

Walks 13 and 14

Walks 13 and 14 give two options for circular walks that can be commenced in Haworth village, or just over two kilometres to the west, using the car parks off Moor Side Lane. This road runs between Stanbury and Oxenhope to the west of Haworth and has several locations where cars can be parked safely.

We will give you the route from Haworth centre, so if you drive the first part of the walk, just pick up the route at the relevant location. Walk 13 is the longer option, at around fifteen kilometres, (eight miles) and includes Withins Heights and Top Withins, whilst Walk 14 is around five kilometres less. Both walks can be reduced by a further four kilometres by parking off Moor Side Lane.

Walk 13

We suggest that you leave Haworth town centre by the path that commences between The Black Bull and Haworth's church of St Michael and All Angels. Walking through the graveyard and away from the church to the south-west continue passed Weavers Lane Car Park in what was Jagger's Quarry, then take a right turn (west). This well maintained lane crosses another minor road where you take the south-west fork towards Penistone Hill.

Keep walking south-west towards Haworth West End Cricket Club. Walking westerly, you now pass a number of car parks accessible from Moor Side Lane, so those wanting to skip this first section can park here and pick up the route.

Once over Moor Side Lane, follow the boundary track passed Drop Farm, which is also the route of the Millennium Way Circular Walk. Leeshaw Reservoir is at a lower level to your left (south), and Haworth Moor on the higher ground to your right. Continue walking for three kilometres south-west from Moor Side Lane and steadily gain height to Oxenhope Stoop Hill. Keep to the higher ground for another kilometre due west to Dick Delf Hill, after which you will meet the Pennine Way long distance trail running from the south-west to the north-east.

The moor is quite featureless in this area, so use the clearly defined Pennine Way as your marker when you need to change direction to the north. Withins Heights is to the north-west and the ruin of Top Withins Farm is just a short distance north along the Pennine Way. If it is a calm day, then enjoy the splendour of this wild location for a rest. Should the wind be rather biting, then wait a while, as the area around the Brontë Waterfall is more sheltered.

Take care to follow the correct path easterly from Top Withins. The Pennine Way heads north-east, you want to head to your right (easterly), losing height and soon crossing a tributary to South Dean Beck. Stay on this path, not taking the path south to Harbour Hill, (which is to your right). Keeping South Dean Beck to your right, continue along the hillside for a kilometre until another path south is taken.

This path leads down the slope to Brontë Bridge, over South Dean Beck and with the Brontë Waterfall due south. This is an ideal location for a refreshment stop, with the peaty streams flowing by, the rich green valley, an attractive footbridge and the waterfall. Again, we know from diaries and letters that this was a walk and location that the Brontë children would often take from the Parsonage, a little over three kilometres away. You will also find here a large chair-shaped stone now named the Brontë chair.

Seeing the waterfall in full spate is a wonderful sight but in the summer months it is often little more than a trickle. Sladen Beck runs east from the Brontë Bridge through the delightful valley and the whole area is a beautiful spot which the Brontës greatly enjoyed in all weathers at all times of the year.

For this walk, head back from the Brontë Bridge, walking almost due east along Enfield Side Road, which, after starting as a footpath, becomes a wider track for most of its length. It begins with a short climb from the Brontë Bridge and then a two kilometre walk, keeping generally level along the south side of the valley. The ground falls away to your left (north) with Sladen Beck which now flows into Lower Laithe Reservoir. The track is increasingly well made up as it allows access to several farms, some in ruin, and a few converted in to houses whose inhabitants have the pleasure of the wonderful views over the valley.

On reaching Moor Side Lane, cross over and head for Penistone Hill. Unless you left your car here, cross Dimples Lane and pick up the many tracks leading back to Haworth Church and your starting point. A pleasant half day walk that has taken you to some of the well-known landmarks of Haworth Moor.

Walk 14

This walk has the same start and finish location as Walk 13 and can also be commenced from the car parks off Moor Side Lane, but is shorter than the first walk. This is achieved by taking the same paths passed Haworth Cricket Club, over Moor Side Lane and passing Drop Farm.

Less than a kilometre west of Drop Farm, leave Walk 13 at a fork that takes you due west, slowly gaining height. With the path now joining a track, Wether Hill is ahead. This track leads to Harbour Lodge but you take another path to the north. This will shortly cross over the beck which forms the Bronte waterfall and you will start to lose height as you descend down to the Bronte Bridge.

The path meets our longer Walk 13 at Brontë Bridge. Both these streams flow over a series of waterfalls as they rapidly lose height in this wonderful setting. You need to be heading east from this site, gaining height prior to reaching Enfield Side Road. Follow this track passed Far Intake and then Middle Intake Farm, where for Walk 13 you would fork right and head south east back to Moor Side Lane.

Crossing this lane, pick up the many paths that head for Penistone Hill and then cross Dimples Lane and on to the church. A pleasant walk of around ten kilometres, (six miles) which taking it at a steady pace, will be around three hours.

Fact File – Walks 13 and 14: Haworth to Brontë Bridge and Waterfall Circular.

Start/Finish – Grid ref: SE 030 373, (or Moor Side Lane, SE 018 362)

OS Maps: OL21 (1:25,000), Landranger 103 and 104 (1:50,000)

Start/finish: The Black Bull, Main Street, Haworth, or you can use Moor Side Lane, 2km west of Haworth, to reduce your walk by 4km.

General Information – a few steep hills and exposed moorland paths, walk 13 is 14km, allow over 3-4 hours, (we recommend you check the weather forecast before you commence walking over the moors). Walk 14 is around 10km, allow up to 3 hours. Plenty of food and toilet facilities around Haworth town centre. Toilets on Moor Side Lane, though not always open.

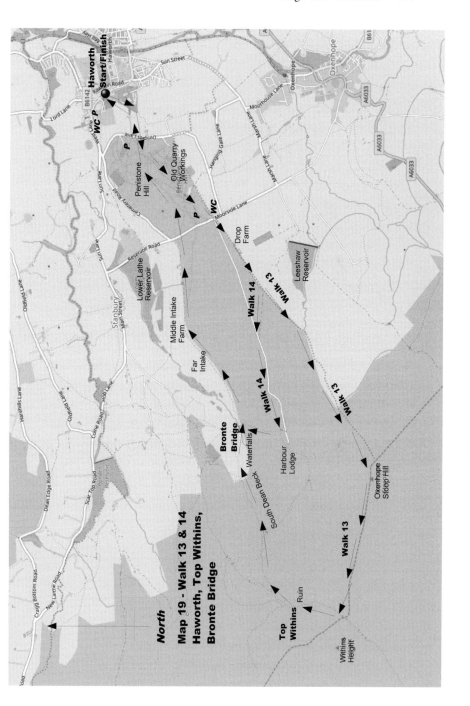

North

**Map 19 - Walk 13 & 14
Haworth, Top Withins,
Bronte Bridge**

Above and below: Such is the worldwide extent of the Brontës' reputation that a number of the signs across Haworth Moors are in Japanese, in honour and recognition of the number of tourists who make the long journey to Haworth.

Above: Over Penistone Hill and passed the old quarry workings, as you venture out onto Haworth Moors.

Below: The track is well defined as you head westwards, but in inclement weather you will need your map and compass when out on the moors.

Above: There is further parking areas off Moor Side Lane, if you do not want to walk the first section of this trail.

Below: For a longer walk, continue straight on, or if heading along the shorter distance to Brontë Falls, fork right at this way marker.

The path is not as clear as you head west, but way markers are to be found to confirm your route.

A moorland path leading down from Top Withins to Brontë Bridge. The ruin of Top Withins is just visible on the skyline.

The beauty and the bleakness of the open moors is so clear from this view, not far from Withins Heights. Even in good weather, navigation can be tricky, so keep looking at your large-scale map.

Above: Ancient pavers mark this section of one of the paths across the moors, keeping you off the boggy ground.

Below: Looking south from Withins Heights, the Pennine Way passes here and many walkers are to be seen throughout the year, most walking south to north.

Above: Having just crossed the tributary of South Dean Beck, looking back, up towards Top Withins.

Below: Looking downstream at the wonderful setting of Brontë Bridge. Cross over the bridge and take the path leading due east, back towards Haworth. The Brontë waterfall is to your right.

Chapter 16

Haworth to Lumb Foot and along the river Worth, circular

Walk 15

One of the many beauties of the Haworth area is that you do not necessarily require transport to head for the start of your walk. This circular trek of around three to four kilometres can be commenced from the north side of the village, taking two possible options of a clockwise walk of one to two hours.

The start point is the narrow lane off North Street, opposite Changegate Car Park. The first part of this walk is along footpaths at the rear of some properties and includes walking by the three small cemeteries of the Methodist and Baptist chapels, on West Lane. Walking in a westerly direction, you are making for Lower Oldfield Farm just under a kilometre from your start location.

You will pass two other paths to the south that go back to Haworth, but you will continue walking west, losing height as you head for the river Worth. Like many of the walks in this book, livestock are regularly in the fields and moorland so please keep any dogs, or excited young children, under appropriate control.

Once you have crossed the river Worth you have various paths to choose from. The path to your right doubles back on itself and takes you along the north bank of the river Worth. This can be followed walking easterly for a kilometre all the way to Lord Lane, where you will turn right and back up the hill to Haworth village. We suggest taking the left option and to keep walking west towards Lumbfoot

Road. This is a beautiful area with the river never far away and lots of trees and foliage, flowers and birds.

Passing a few farm buildings on your right-hand side, you need to be looking out for a path to the right (north) and leading through a wooded area. Lumbfoot Road crosses over the river and straight into the village of Lumb Foot. If that route is taken, you will be walking back up the hill towards Stanbury cemetery and Sun Lane, just under two kilometres west of Haworth village.

If you choose the alternative route, now walking northwards, you have an incline for 200 metres towards Hey Lane. The different permutations to your route options are high and, as always, we would encourage you to study your maps and seek out new routes following public footpaths and bridleways. For this walk, you will turn right where the wooded area ends and head in a generally easterly direction.

Again, with several options, we suggest you cross over Lumbfoot Road and return down towards the river Worth. Taking the path before the bridge over the river, you pick up the route that runs along the north side or the river Worth and walk all the way to Lord Lane. As described above, walk up Lord Lane (there is a path at the roadside, so it's safe if you're with children) towards Haworth and your start point to this walk at North Street.

This is not the longest walk in the book, but for a leisurely circular stroll of one to two hours (depending which route you take), this is a nice way to spend an afternoon. Some parts can be a little muddy after heavy rain.

Lumb Foot is an attractive hamlet with a slightly chequered recent history. Once dominated by its worsted mill with its weaving and spinning sheds, it is now a residential area which declared independence from the UK in 1989 and became twinned with Lhasa in Tibet!

Fact File – Walk 15: Haworth to Lumb Foot and along the river Worth, circular.

Start/Finish – Grid ref: SE 028 374

OS Maps: OL21 (1:25,000), Landranger 104 (1:50,000)

Start/finish: Changegate Car Park, North Street, Haworth.

General Information – a few gentle hills and field paths, can be a little muddy. Please keep dogs under firm control, as much of this route has livestock in the fields. Short section of road walking, but with good footpath. Plenty of food and toilet facilities around Haworth town centre.

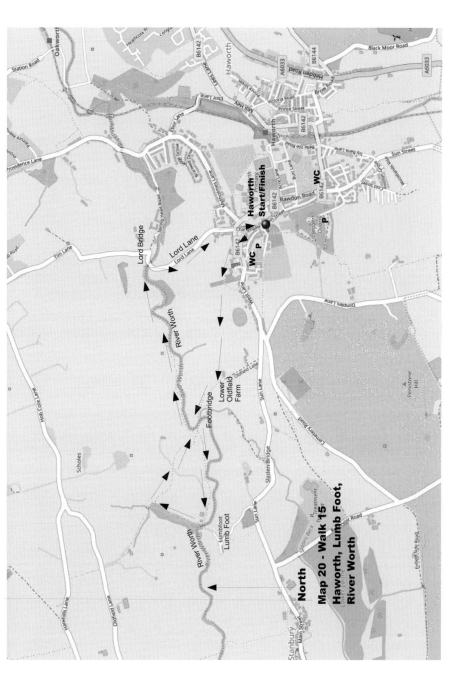

Map 20 - Walk 15 - Haworth, Lumb Foot, River Worth

Above: Typical of the paths heading west out of Haworth towards Lumb Foot. Remember to keep your pets on a short lead, as most of these field contain livestock.

Below: This attractive stone bridge takes you over the River Worth, just over a kilometre west of Haworth.

Above: Wonderful tranquil paths through the fields by the River Worth, not far from Lumb Foot.

Below: Looking down to Lumb Foot with the River Worth below and your route through the line of trees on the opposite side of the valley.

Above: Way marker to Lumb Foot.

Below: Pavers mark the route of the path, looking back towards The Parsonage. This route is described in several of our walks taking ramblers from The Parsonage to West Lane.

Chapter 17

Haworth to Brontë Bridge, Oldfield and river Worth, circular

Walk 16

The selection of countryside walks that make up this chapter, can also start/finish in Haworth centre, but there are plenty of options to park a few kilometres to the west, if you wish to shorten your route. There is also a little road walking which links the various paths into one circular route. Although only a short time is spent road walking, you may wish to look at other options if you have small children in your party or a large group that can be difficult to manage. When short sections of the walks are on narrow roads without a fully made up path, you should always face the oncoming traffic; it is wise to wear a brightly coloured top and to keep a sharp lookout for oncoming vehicles. We would also remind motorists in the countryside to drive at a speed that enables you to react appropriately if you sight walkers or cyclists on narrow, winding, and sometimes icy, country lanes.

To start in Haworth, you will commence from outside The Black Bull inn, by the steps leading up to St Michael and All Angles Church. Walk by the north side of the church and along Church Street. Pass the Parsonage on your left and keep going west until Church Street becomes a field path. Cross the small field towards the north-west corner and out on to the road. This is West Lane and you need to turn left and take the immediate left fork which is Cemetery Road.

There are several locations where you can park along this road, if you wish to avoid the first section of the walk out of the town centre.

There is less than a kilometre of road walking but keep a sharp lookout for vehicles. The road is narrow in places. You will pass the entrance to the large cemetery on your left, opened in the late nineteenth century as a final result of the Babbage report of 1850. Lower Laithe Reservoir (opened 1925) dominates the view ahead with elevated views to your right across the valley. The village of Oldfield is visible on the opposite slopes.

On reaching Moor Side Lane, cross over and take the track heading due west and signed to Brontë Waterfalls and Top Withins. It is a wide track and easy to follow, passing a number of old farms along the route. Some are converted into pleasant dwellings, whilst others are in a semi-derelict state. This track also forms part of the Brontë Way and is around two kilometres from Moor Side Lane before dropping down to Brontë Bridge.

The streams converge at this location, having tumbled over the falls upstream. Cross over the narrow stone bridge and head north, climbing up the steep bank. One path leads west to Top Withins, and several paths head north, but take the one clearly marked 'Brontë Way'. This crosses several east-west routes, as it takes you over the brow and then steadily descending towards Buckley Green. Turn to the east at this location and pass by the cottage which was the dwelling of the last known traditional home weaver, Timothy Feather.

The Brontë Way takes the route north-west at this location, but you should head east. Now walking on a wide track, it is a few hundred metres to Cold Knowle End Farm where you turn north again. This path zig-zags north and east over the small fields and down to Hob Lane, next to the river Worth. There are often horses or sheep in these fields but as long as you have any dogs under firm control, they should not bother you.

At Hob Lane, turn left to cross the bridge over the river Worth then take the path north, at the opposite side of the road. Set off along the riverside for just a short distance, then it is a north-east track, gaining height towards the cluster of dwellings called Oldfield. Most of the paths in this book are quite well waymarked, but several signs are currently missing from this section of the walk. Have your map to hand, as this will aid you to find the gaps in the walls and fences, where the path heads north-east. Pass Oldfield End Farm, with the path running parallel to Oldfield Lane, a short distance to the north. If you get stuck you can always walk along the lane for a short section.

Pass West House Farm and then Street Head Farm, where you need to take the path heading south-east down the hill known as Street Lane. Stay on the path heading south-east, as you pass over a steep-sided stream. The path to your right heads alongside this stream, through the trees and down to Lumb Foot at the other side of the river Worth.

Continue south-east, crossing over another track, (called Lumbfoot Road) and head down the hill to the river bank. No fewer than five footpaths converge around this point but you will head over the attractive stone arch bridge, and start to gain height again. Walk up to Lower Oldfield Farm and take your choice of two directions. Depending where you started your walk, if your transport is near the cemetery, head up the track to your right, called Oldfield Lane, which takes you up to Sun Lane very close to its junction with Cemetery Road.

If heading for The Black Bull Inn, continue along the path to the north side of the dwelling and along a series of paths, almost due east. You approach the north end of Haworth behind the properties fronting West Lane. Cemeteries are to each side of the path and you have the option to take a path south, to arrive at West Lane, close to The Old Sun Inn. The main path continues all the way passed the back of West Lane Baptist Centre to finally arrive at North Street, opposite Changegate car park.

Taking the full circular route, you will have covered around eight kilometres, (five miles) with a few steep sections out on the moors.

Fact File – Walk 16: Haworth to Brontë Bridge, Oldfield and river Worth, circular.

Start/Finish – Grid ref: SE 030 373, (or SE 022 372 – Cemetery Road).

OS Maps: OL21 (1:25,000), Landranger 104 (1:50,000)

Start/finish: Black Bull Inn, Main Street, Haworth.

General Information – a good mix of field paths, tracks and open moors with some steep sections over a circular route of 8km. You can reduce the length to 6km, if parking along Cemetery Road. Muddy in parts, so boots recommended, along with a good map, as some way markers are missing, especially around Oldfield. Please keep your dog under close control, as many sections of this route have livestock in the fields. Some road walking, but with good footpaths. Plenty of food and toilet facilities around Haworth town centre.

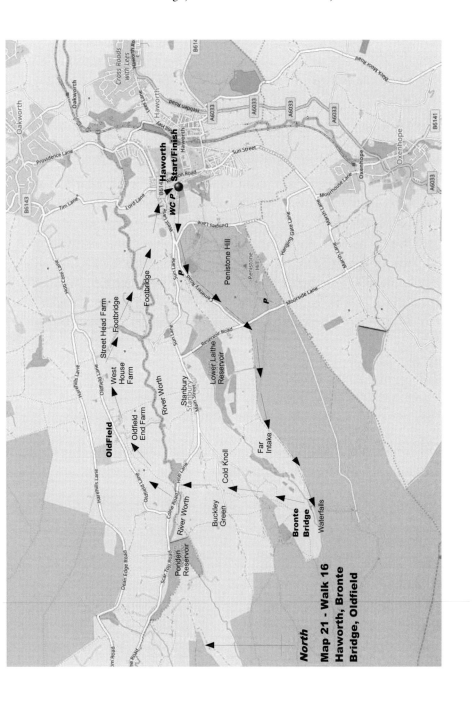

Map 21 - Walk 16
Haworth, Bronte
Bridge, Oldfield

Above and below: The path is both well-defined and has clear signage as you head away from Haworth towards Brontë Falls and Bridge.

Above: The view north from the path towards Stanbury, with Oldfield in the distance.

Below: View approaching Brontë Bridge from the east.

Above: Having approached Brontë Bridge from the east, cross over the structure and head north up the steep hill.

Below: Follow the way marker north towards Stanbury and beyond to Oldfield.

Above: Looking back (south), over South Dean Beck to Brontë Falls tumbling down the opposite hillside.

Right: Not every way marker stands out and this one on Hob Lane, west of Stanbury, is well camouflaged.

Looking east the footpaths run parallel to Oldfield Lane. Keep your large scale map to hand as some sections are not well way-marked.

In the summer months the paths become overgrown but way markers can be spotted if you look closely, as with this one just north of Lumb Foot, on Hey Lane.

Heading south-easterly back down to the River Worth.

Chapter 18

Railways: the Worth Valley Railway and circular walks

Haworth to Keighley, Walks 17 and 18

Change is something that modern man has become used to and sees as inevitable, though often challenging. The speed of technological development in the twenty-first century is unprecedented and it creates its own momentum. It is therefore a bold statement to suggest that over the lifespan of the Rev. Patrick Brontë, he would have witnessed possibly the greatest social, agricultural and industrial changes Britain had experienced throughout its history, up to that time.

Born into poverty in County Down, Ireland, Patrick Brontë moved from a mainly rural existence in 1777 to one at the heart of the industrial revolution in 1861, the year of his death. This century of change affected everyone at all levels of social class and altered the entire landscape of Britain. In Yorkshire, a person's employment no longer depended exclusively on his or her class and their ability to work the land or produce goods at home. The growth of industry meant that people could produce more within a factory setting, or from a mine or a quarry. A population that traditionally would have ventured no further than a few kilometres around their own village, took advantage of a developing national transport system which could move hundreds of people and goods at relatively high speeds throughout the country. This had never been possible before and presented opportunities for people to travel and change their lifestyles and occupations.

Communication via the telegraph (1837) and the spread of national newspapers meant that news and events could be distributed and communicated to nearly all of the population. Information, education and business was creating wealth and opening up the rest of the world to trade and development, though not without conflict. Patrick Brontë observed and experienced many aspects of this and the upset in religious faith and observance which it engendered.

This time of change and upheaval can be viewed from both an aesthetic and a commercial stance. Whilst the new infrastructure brought employment and wealth it destroyed the countryside in ways that would never be restored. At the end of her novel *Shirley*, Charlotte Brontë highlights a conversation between the entrepreneurial mill owner, Robert Moore and his future wife, Caroline Helstone, where he boasts of tearing up the countryside to build a huge mill. Their conversation runs as follows:

'The copse shall be firewood ere five years elapse: the beautiful wild ravine shall be a smooth descent; the green natural terrace shall be a paved street: there shall be cottages in the dark ravine, and cottages on the lonely slopes: the rough pebbled track shall have an even, firm, broad, black, sooty road, bedded with the cinders from my mill: and my mill, Caroline – my mill shall fill its present yard.'

'Horrible! You will change our blue hill-country air into the Stilbro' smoke atmosphere.'

'I will pour the waters of Pactolus through the valley of Briarfield.'

'I like the beck a thousand times better.'

'I will get an act for enclosing Nunnely Common, and parcelling it out in to farms.'

'Stilbro' Moor, however, defies you, thank Heaven! What can you grow in Bilberry Moss! What will flourish on Rushedge?'

'Caroline, the houseless, the starving, the unemployed, shall come to Hallow's Mill from far and near; and Joe Scott shall give them work, and Louis Moore, Esq., shall let them a tenement, and Mrs Gill shall mete them a portion till the first pay-day'

Charlotte Brontë, *Shirley*

As it was then, so it is now, when we are battling with such controversial changes as fracking, windfarms and housing shortages. How much pillage of the land is progress and how much is destruction? It all depends where your priorities and needs lie.

Of all the inventions and developments, one could argue that from a commercial and social perspective none made such an impact, and at every level, than that of the railways. First across Britain, then exported around the globe, railways allowed people to travel and function in a wholly different way. From a fragmented transport system that only served the more affluent and which was slow, uncomfortable, without reliability and in many aspects dangerous, it grew into a means of travel for all. It also allowed for the movement of vast amounts of raw materials and finished goods and produce.

It is hard to comprehend just how significant the railways were and how they changed the whole way of life in such a relatively short time span. From just a few thousand kilometres of canals, the nation was criss-crossed with over 30,000 kilometres (21,000 miles) of railway routes, connecting almost every community in the British Isles. The speed of change was overwhelming, with thousands of people moving from their rural lives of subsistence to work in factories, mills, mines and industries across the nation. This created the large towns and cities but with the overcrowding and disease that accompanied such rapid expansion.

At the heart of all this developing commerce was the railway, so it is appropriate that we talk about its impact on the Brontës, even though the local Worth valley line did not fully open until April 1867, six years after Patrick's death in 1861. Trains first arrived in Leeds in 1834, into Bradford from July 1846 and Keighley from March 1847, and these lines were all used by the Brontës during these years. However, the Keighley line was only available to Emily and Anne for the last two years of their lives. The sisters regularly walked to Keighley and back, a distance of thirteen kilometres, (eight miles) and took a cart to Leeds or Bradford stations if they were travelling further.

It is for this reason we detail the local railway development and try to help you to appreciate the changes that the Brontës were experiencing. The sisters, like most other people, would have found it almost impossible to travel any distance away from their hometown without this new developing transport network. The railways speeded up important communication systems. Mail would arrive more quickly, along with newspapers, spreading news of all manner of new and exciting political, social and commercial events and prospects. Centuries of social isolation were being superseded by a huge, new network of communication and information.

It is important to remember that new and exciting though the railways were – and more reliable and capable than horse-drawn vehicles or canal travel – they were also dirty, noisy, relatively slow and uncomfortable. Some people found them obnoxious and a blight on the countryside and did not appreciate the amount and speed of change taking place around them. The journey from Leeds to London in 1840 could take up to twelve hours and whilst this was an enormous improvement, it was still a long and tedious ride for the traveller.

Even many landowners and gentry were initially averse to railway development as they saw it as a threat to their power over their workers. The railway gave people the option to find employment elsewhere and moved them away from the land. However, as the network grew and the advantages were recognised, many wealthy people invested in railway shares and tried to dictate routes and stations that served their own purposes.

Today's heritage railways attempt to recreate for the twenty-first-century traveller a means to experience and appreciate active history and although in a rather 'clinical' atmosphere, you can imagine you are travelling in the past as you take your train journeys along country routes in restored carriages pulled by steam engines. Most of these heritage lines set a theme around the 1930s, which is naturally a century later than the Brontë siblings, but you can experience a different pace of life and learn how so much evolved around the railways and the local stations, in a manner reminiscent of early railway travel.

Thanks to the many thousands of hours spent by volunteers across the country, heritage railway lines have proved to be a magnet for experiencing 'living history' and the Worth valley route was an early success story in this type of venture. The line, from its terminus at Keighley to Oxenhope, six kilometres (four miles) away was closed in 1961. This was before the Beeching era, when Dr Richard Beeching introduced his infamous report which brought about the closure of around half of the route mileage of railways across the British Isles. This was implemented by British Railways from 1963 onwards.

Almost immediately after the closure of the Keighley to Oxenhope line, an enthusiastic group of locals looked into retaining the infrastructure of the railway. This was particularly critical, as once the rails and any key engineering structures are removed re-opening becomes a massive task, way beyond the scope of most volunteer groups.

Lengthy discussions took place and eventually agreement was reached for the sale of the assets to the new company and work began in earnest to open the route as a heritage railway. After much hard work, the line re-opened in the summer of 1968. It is important to stress the term 'heritage railway', as such lines operate very differently to the national railway network. They are strictly governed for reasons of public safety and are not permitted to travel over 25mph, (around 40kmph). They exist for tourists to gain insight and knowledge of this era of railway dominance, when every significant village, town, factory or mine would be connected to the national railway network.

The Worth Valley Railway operates throughout the year, but naturally there is a lot more activity over the summer months and during many themed weekend events. The passenger services can also be used to link together walks along the route of the line, removing the need to do a circular walk, back to your means of transport.

Walk 6, (covered in chapter 11), detailed a circular walk from Haworth station to Oxenhope station, returning via Field Head. Our next series of walks cover the area to the north of Haworth station, towards Oakworth and then on to Damems, Ingrow and finally to the centre of Keighley.

Like Walk 6, our next ramble (Walk 17) can be made into a circular trek by foot, or by using the train for one leg of the journey. You will start at Haworth station and head north to Oakworth station. There is some road walking to link the various paths, but well worth it to enjoy some splendid views along Bridgehouse Beck and the river Worth.

If you are starting from one of the car parks at either end of Main Street, head for Butt Lane, which leads down to the footbridge over the railway lines by Haworth station. Before the footbridge, take a left turn in to Mill Hill. If you are already at the station, then head up the long ramp and over the footbridge towards Butt Lane. Once reaching Butt Lane take the right-hand junction in to Mill Hill. After a short distance north, turn left into Acre Lane. Continue for a short distance and a footpath will take you north over the playing fields with Haworth Primary School over to your left.

Keep heading north (not taking the path to the left) towards Greenfields cul-de-sac and Mytholmes Lane. Turn right along this road and follow it just a few hundred metres to Ebor Lane. Pass this lane on the right but take the path immediately after the junction, also on the right. This track will reduce the amount of road walking but we also highlight a slightly longer route on the map which, by staying on the main road, now called Victoria Avenue, leads into Providence Lane.

Back to your walk, head over the railway line once again close to the southern portal of the short tunnel. This is a thickly wooded area with plenty of habitat for wildlife and never far from flowing water. Keep following the meandering track which takes you over the beck and close to where it is joined by the river Worth to your left. Also to the left is the railway line, now emerged from the short tunnel and onto an embankment, taking a long sweeping curve and crossing three bridges in quick succession over the river Worth.

This section of the railway was completely rebuilt in the 1880s, as originally it was on a line slightly further to the east with a long section carried on a wooden trestle viaduct. To improve the track and increase capacity, the new tunnel was constructed and also the embankment to the north, on a long curve which includes the three new river bridges.

Back on your walk, another path joins you from the right (which is your route back to Haworth station) and you then meet Vale Mill Lane, where you turn left to walk along this narrow road. Still with the railway on a gentle bend round to the left, you head down the road and over the river Worth by Vale Mill. This is a sharp blind corner so do beware of traffic movement and the sounding of vehicle horns.

The river disappears under the road and part of the large stone-built Vale Mill and was no doubt the source of power before the days of steam. At the sharp corner, a steep path heads straight ahead and under the railway line and then joins up with the longer route described earlier, from Providence Lane. Take a right turn onto this steep path and take care as it can be very slippery.

Back next to Vale Mill, it is only a short distance along the lane and passed the mill building on your right to Oakworth station. The road crosses the railway line at a level crossing and the station buildings are on the right-hand side. The steep path route meets this road (now aptly named Station Road) just a short distance further along.

You now have a number of options. You can take the train from Oakworth station north to Keighley, or south back to Haworth, or walk back to Haworth to complete a circular walk of just over four kilometres. Alternatively, continue on foot to Damems station, Ingrow station and Keighley station where the Worth Valley Railway terminates.

For the walk back to Haworth, return passed Vale Mill buildings and back onto the path at the second sharp corner. This time take the path on the left after approximately one hundred metres (so staying at the east side of the railway and beck). This takes you through the thickly wooded area, never far from the Bridgehouse Beck, for several hundred metres. Parts of this path can be very wet as it is located between stone walls, trapping large puddles of water. Finally, the beck is crossed by a footbridge and with the railway on your right and another large mill complex on your left, you arrive at Ebor Lane. The chimney of Ebor Mill can be viewed to the east and is a reminder of the hundreds of mill chimneys that once dominated the landscape at so many industrial locations across the north of England.

Ebor Mill began life as a water-powered spinning mill around 1820 and by 1887 it had grown into a five storey textile mill. Like many mills, the combination of combustible materials, heat, and poor Health and Safety measures, meant that it suffered a series of devastating fires. The last was in August 2014, which totally destroyed the buildings and now only the chimney remains.

Turn left along this road and over the beck to join Mill Hey Road, which is the B6142. Turn right along this road and back towards Haworth station which comes into view on your right-hand side, having again crossed over Bridgehouse Beck.

There is plenty to see around the station area and naturally plenty of facilities for food, drink and toilets. The footbridge to the south of the station can lead you over the railway and up the steep hill (Butt Lane) towards the town centre with its further array of shops, hotels and of course the Brontë Parsonage and church.

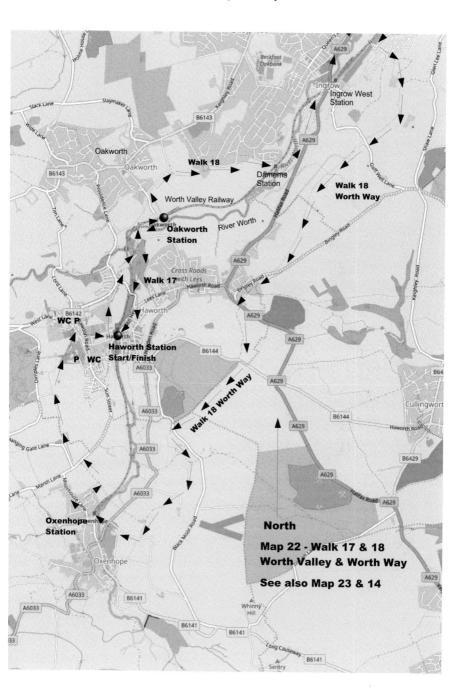

Above: Looking east down Butt Lane towards the railway station. These cobbles become very slippery when wet, do take care.

Below: A tranquil day at Haworth Station on the Worth Valley Line, viewed from the footbridge.

Right: The Worth Way is generally well signed throughout.

Below: Oakworth Station on a damp day with a permanent way team working on the well kept track, at the east side of the station.

An original gas lantern at Oakworth Station is beautifully decorated with hanging plants tended by local volunteers.

Above: Your route takes you across the level crossing west of Oakworth Station.

Below: The Worth Valley Railway is bridged over the River Worth at this location, west of Vale Mill.

Above: The tracks sweep around to the south portal of the only tunnel on the Worth Valley line, between Haworth and Oakworth.

Right: Although the undergrowth is thick, the path is easy to follow back to Haworth.

Above: Looking south, a short distance north of Haworth Station where the Worth Valley Railway is bridged, next to the former site of the Ebor Mill.

Left: A monument to the past, as the former Ebor Mill's chimney dominates this part of the view. Dozens of such chimneys littered the skyline in the Brontës' time, with each one emitting clouds of thick smoke from the roaring furnace below.

Walk 18

For those venturing further by foot, return to Oakworth station and continue your walk, (now Walk 18), the 1½ kilometres to Damems station. Turn right out of Oakworth station, along Station Road towards Oakworth village centre. It is around 200 metres up the hill before you take the next path on the right, which is found by walking along East Royd towards Cackleshaw. If you wish to visit the Oakworth village centre or walk around Holden Park, it is only another 300 metres further along Station Road and Park Avenue.

Back on your path, this leaves East Royd on your right-hand side where the lane takes a left bend. The path is well used as it forms part of the Worth Way and is not difficult to follow. It is around 500 metres to the east from Station Road to Harewood Hill. You enter Damems village on Goose Cote Lane, still walking in an easterly direction. Goose Cote Lane turns to the left and becomes Bracken Bank Avenue, where a track off to the right should be taken. This is Damems Lane and after 300 metres walking down the slope will bring you to Damems station; another station on the Worth Valley Railway and another option of catching the train, or continuing on foot towards Ingrow and then onwards to Keighley. Damems station is only a small halt, so does not offer all the facilities of the larger stations along the Worth valley line. Continue your walk by crossing over the railway line at the level crossing and almost immediately over the river Worth. Damems Lane continues straight on but you will take the left turn along Damems Road. This is a wide track running parallel to the river Worth on your left, with the railway line on the opposite bank of the river. After a few hundred metres you can stay close to the riverbank on footpaths or, if very wet, remain on Damems Road. Both are heading north-east towards Ingrow West station, not far now from Keighley. Though hidden by undergrowth and an embankment to your right, the course of another dismantled railway from Halifax is also running parallel to Damems Road.

Ingrow was the location where the Great Northern Railway's line from Halifax, via Queensbury, joined the Worth Valley Railway. The track bed is sandwiched between Damems Road and the busy A629 Halifax Road, both to your right. This was a heavily engineered railway line built to provide a route north from Halifax towards Keighley and beyond. Prior to the Worth Valley Railway being opened, many local businessmen had hoped that the Worth valley line would have formed part of a railway south to Halifax and then across the Pennines. This would have allowed more rail traffic to use the Worth valley route as part of a main line railway, rather than a short branch line.

Instead, the Worth valley route was built as a branch line south from Keighley and although being a great asset to Haworth, Oxenhope and the surrounding villages and mills, it would always be vulnerable when road traffic became dominant during the mid-twentieth century. The Great Northern route fared little better with Queensbury, the principal town on the route, having the station located a long way from the town and without a proper access road. Add to this, the great cost of upkeep to the succession of viaducts and tunnels needed along the route, this line also succumbed to closure, along with the line that ran from the triangular layout of Queensbury station direct to Bradford.

Back to your route from Damems station, you continue along the paths at the side of the river Worth and reach Grove Mill Drive. The Damems Road route has now joined the busy A629, called Westley Place, and is still running parallel though further east of the river. Both routes cross the railway line and merge next to Ingrow West station, located at the other side (east) of the A629, with the large Prospect Mills complex at the west side of the road.

This is now very much a part of the urban sprawl of Keighley, though there is the best part of another two kilometres before you reach the terminus at Keighley station. You are now mainly in an industrial setting where the banks of the river Worth hold a wealth of industrial heritage. Many large cloth mills occupied sites along its course. All the mills of this nature required vast amounts of clean water to process the wool and, in earlier days, it was the waterwheels that provided the power to operate the mill machinery.

Ingrow West station has many interesting features for the curious visitor. A museum is located here and includes the carriage works, engine shed and a learning coach, along with the station buildings. A small charge is made but it houses several notable collections of rolling stock, all well laid out for the visitor. The station buildings are not the original structures from the Worth Valley Railway; it was rebuilt, stone by stone, from the demolished Foulridge station in Lancashire in 1989.

To the east of the station complex, though now completely dismantled, was the Ingrow East station of the Great Northern Railway. Only someone with a keen eye will spot the walls of the original parapets of the bridge taking Haincliffe Road over the former railway lines.

You cannot avoid the next few hundred metres of road walking. You can take South Street, which forms part of the A629 to the west, or Hainworth Wood Road North, at the east side. Both have wide footpaths but the main road into Keighley is naturally very busy with traffic. Walk to Woodhouse Road then along this lane and down to the bridge over the river Worth. Immediately east of this bridge, take the steps down to the path at the side of the river Worth, with the railway line at your right-hand side. It is still just over a kilometre to Keighley station and requires two crossings under the railway line before you reach Low Mill Lane, where you will cross over the river Worth again. This section of the path is sandwiched between walls and the river, and then between two high walls. The railway is on one side with first the river Worth, then a series of factory walls on the other side. This does lead to the path feeling very enclosed; lacking a view and home to both litter and undergrowth.

Keep walking north to Park Lane, which crosses over the river Worth on your left and under the Worth Valley Railway on a girder bridge to your right. Do not take the road under the railway bridge, but cross over Park Lane with care and walk through the small brick arch at the side of the girder bridge. The path takes an immediate left turn, to hug the railway line for a short distance at the other side of the arch, still heading north.

A zig-zag right, then left, takes you over a girder bridge that takes the path over the very overgrown track bed of the former Great Northern Railway's lines. No sooner over this bridge, you head through a stone arch taking you under the tracks of the Worth Valley Railway once again, to now cling to the west side of the railway route the last few hundred metres into Keighley station. This is a disappointing last section of what has been a beautiful walk for most of the length. You are again sandwiched between the railway at a higher level to your right and a stone wall to your left, leaving the walker to step tentatively over broken slabs of stone, a disappointing amount of rubbish, plus an array of nettles, brambles and bushes. Some would argue that industrial landscapes are never stunning but we would differ in our view. Such heritage can have its own beauty, although nothing is enhanced by endless litter. This is a well-used path that encourages many visitors to the town but could be greatly improved with more attention.

With the railway curving around to the north-west the path meets Low Mill Lane. Do not go through the railway bridge on your right, but follow this lane over the river Worth and Keighley Railway station is on your right-hand side. The station adjoins the mainline Airedale Railway route, with trains north to Skipton, Settle and Carlisle, and south-east to Leeds and Bradford, Forster Square station. The main station frontage faces Bradford Road where you gain access to both the Worth Valley Railway and the Leeds, Settle and Carlisle route. Naturally plenty of facilities are available both at the railway station and in the town centre.

It is interesting to note that the present Keighley station is not the original one. A station existed across Bradford Road opposite the current station in what is now a collection of railway sidings, buildings and the ASDA superstore. The original station was built here in 1847 and would have been used by the Brontë family. This station was still standing when the Worth Valley Railway was opened in 1867. When the Great Northern Railway line came to Keighley in the 1880s a whole new station complex was constructed and it involved moving the passenger station to the east side of Bradford Road where it still stands today.

In the early and mid-years of the nineteenth century, Keighley, like many other towns, was expanding with the effects of industrialisation and the influx of workers to the mills. It was also developing in areas of business, commerce and education. Sunday schools, a library and a Mechanics Institute were all founded and these institutions helped to spread information and learning. As Keighley was the nearest large town to Haworth, the Brontë family were frequent visitors for a variety of reasons though they would usually walk here.

The Keighley Mechanics Institute, founded in 1825, had a chequered start when subscriptions waxed and waned and it nearly folded. However, by the mid 1830s it had rallied and eminent speakers came to offer lectures and many books were donated for lending. The Brontë family, including Patrick and Branwell, attended various functions and borrowed books. One evening, when the Rev. William Weightman was giving a lecture, the three Brontë sisters walked to Keighley to hear him and he accompanied them back to the Parsonage around midnight; a long uphill climb in the cold and dark. Aunt Branwell was not amused!

You have the choice of taking the return journey by the train or taking a circular route back to Haworth. For a longer return route you can join the Worth Way footpath to form a circular walk all the way to Oxenhope station. This is a well signposted route but requires retracing your steps one kilometre, next to the railway lines and back to Woodhouse Road. You take a left turn along this road and up the hill to Crag Place where you take the path on your right-hand side and pass

Crag Hill Farm, to your right side. Keep going to the small Kirkstall
Wood, which is passed to the west side and offers a good view behind
you across the urban sprawl of Keighley and the Worth valley.

It is now several kilometres walking south-westerly to Hainworth
Farm and across Hainworth Road towards Hill Top. You still have
good views from this elevated position and maintain your height
passed some extensive old quarry workings on your left. It is many
years since these particular quarries have been worked so the spoil
heaps are now being reclaimed by nature. Parts of the path are a
little overgrown in the summer months but nothing too arduous.
After another kilometre of walking south, you arrive at the village of
Barcroft. The path merges here with Bingley Road and heads to the
busy A625 Halifax Road.

For a quick return downhill to Haworth station, turn right then
left at this location along Haworth Road leading to Lees Lane
(the B6142). Back on the Worth Way and, to avoid walking along the
road, take a left, then cross over Halifax Road to the track leading to
Stump Cross Farm. Known as Hardgate Lane, this leads to Stump
Cross. A short descent is followed by a climb, with another disused
quarry on your left. A path to the right (west) takes you passed the
small reservoir and down towards Haworth Brow. It is then road
walking along the steep descent across the A6033 Hebden Road and
along Brow Road to Haworth town centre.

Back on the path following Hardgate Lane, this route remains on
the Worth Way and to Brow Top Road and is a wide track and easy to
follow. Cross over Brow Top Road (the B6144) and over Brow Moor
and the edge of Cullingworth Moor. The view west is dominated by a
modern wind turbine, so different to the multitude of mill chimneys,
with Haworth town centre beyond. Also to your right is a large
working quarry, though now with massive mechanical excavators,
taking on the role of hundreds of men toiling with picks and shovels.

Cross over Black Moor Road, then walk just a few metres to the sign
pointing to the right stating, The Worth Way. The footpath takes you

down to Lower Naylor Hill Farm and then follows the contours around the hill, passing Delf Hill, North Berks and then Lower Hayley Farm. Have your map handy to guide you to the correct locations where the path passes through gaps in the walls and passed the dwellings along this stretch. Just beyond Lower Hayley Farm, turn right on to Dark Lane and the steady descent across the A6033 Keighley Road. Over this road, continue downhill and to Oxenhope station on your right.

At around nine kilometres (over five miles) from Keighley station, a bracing walk with many fine views, but always with plenty of options to reduce the overall length of the trek, or the use of the train for part of your journey. If you wish to complete the circular walk back to Haworth station, follow Walk 6, detailed in chapter 10, which takes you via Field Head Farm, back to Haworth.

Fact File – Walks 17 and 18: Worth Valley Railway Walks, Haworth to Keighley and circular walk to Oxenhope.

Start/Finish – Grid ref: SE 035 373

OS Maps: OL21 (1:25,000), Landranger 104 (1:50,000)

Start/finish: Haworth Railway station, Station Road, Haworth (B6142), with options to finish at stations along the full route of the Worth Valley Railway.

You can have an hours walk – a mixture of gentle hills, field paths and road walking. With so many route options, you can have an hour's walk between two stations or extend to a circular full day of hiking. If using the train for your return journey, be sure to check the timetable for the day of your walk, as this varies throughout the year. Plenty of food and toilet facilities along the route and at most stations, plus large array of facilities around Haworth and Keighley town centres. Parts of the paths can be muddy, so walking boots are advised, along with your OS map. Contrast the stunning views over most of this route, against a disappointing last kilometre, to the south of Keighley station.

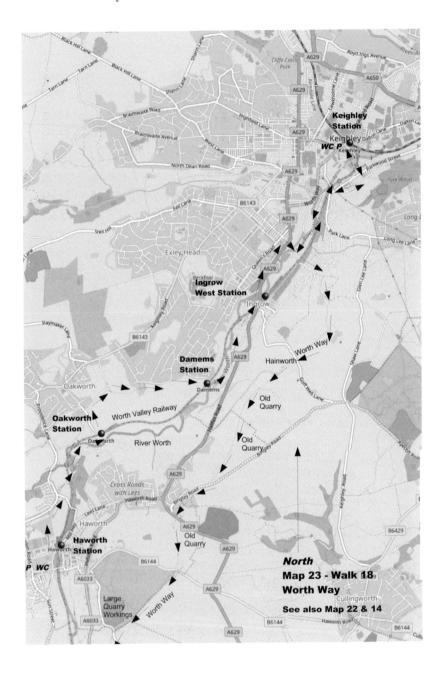

Keighley
Station

Keighley
WC P

Ingrow
West Station

Worth Way

Hainworth

Damems
Station

Old
Quarry

Oakworth
Station

Worth Valley Railway

River Worth

Old
Quarry

Cross Roads
with Lees

Haworth
Station

Old
Quarry

P WC

Large
Quarry
Workings

Worth Way

**North
Map 23 - Walk 18
Worth Way
See also Map 22 & 14**

Above: Looking back from the path to the south west, you can see Vale Mill buildings over the trees and Haworth beyond.

Below: As you snake your way through the housing, helpful way markers guide you along your route.

Above: The steep lane down to the railway level crossing next to Damems Station.

Left: Looking south west along the tracks from Damems level crossing, towards Oakworth.

Above: The compact but well-manicured station at Damems looks deserted on this damp afternoon.

Below: A typical railway warning sign, so common in bygone years along the thousands of miles of rail tracks.

Above: The track is wide as you walk north east alongside the railway and the River Worth between Damems and Ingrow stations.

Left: A sign of the past, close to Ingrow Station, to a day when this location had two stations; one operated by the Midland Railway along the Worth Valley, the other by the Great Northern down to Queensbury, Halifax and Bradford.

Above: The exterior of The Midland railway's Ingrow station, which also houses a small museum at this location.

Below: The north portal of the short Ingrow Tunnel at the end of the station platform.

Above and left: The path, although easy to follow, is now shrouded between high walls, buildings and the railway on an embankment as you near Keighley, so views are greatly restricted.

Above: The Worth Way is now sandwiched between the River Worth on the left and the railway to the right.

Below: You approach this bridge from the right of this view and need to cross this road before heading down the passageway to take you under the railway and the last few hundred metres to Keighley Station.

Above: The Worth Valley Railway sweeps around this curve on its final approach into Keighley Station.

Below: A common site at every railway station until the end of the steam era; a substantial water tank at Keighley Station which would have been used hundreds of times every week, throughout the use of steam powered locomotion.

You cannot hide the rather disappointing finish to a walk that has taken in the beautiful Worth Valley: weeds, broken pavers and rubbish do not enhance the view along the last few metres before Keighley Station.

Not a Midland Railway sign, now Metro heralds the journey's end outside Keighley Station.

Above: You have to be something of a railway historian to spot the clues that the Worth Valley Railway to Haworth and Oxenhope shared the route south of Keighley with the former Great Northern lines to Queensbury. Hidden by over half a century of undergrowth, the former Great Northern route is barely visible under the girder bridge.

Below: More clues that two separate railway routes ran parallel. There are two styles of design to this double railway bridge over the road. One company favoured a stone arch whilst the other chose the slightly more modern girder bridge, nearest to the camera.

Above: Taking a circular route back, you are at a higher level and looking back have a good view over the expanse of Keighley.

Right: Some tidy ballast is viewed on this recently maintained track of the Worth Valley lines, heading south of Keighley.

Above: From your elevated position, the Worth Valley railway snakes along the valley bottom on route for Haworth.

Below: Looking back towards Keighley, there is much evidence of old quarry workings along the east side of the well-defined path.

Chapter 19

Thornton town Trail

Walk 19

We finish our tour of Brontë related walks in the birthplace of four of the Brontë children, in the small town of Thornton. This town lies between Bradford, to the east, and Haworth, around eight kilometres to the north-west. A short stroll of two or three kilometres will take you to several key sites of significance in the Brontë story. The Old Bell Chapel, in which five of the Brontë children were baptised and the Old Parsonage in Market Street, birth place of the four youngest children, which is currently a bistro.

Thornton is six kilometres due west of Bradford city centre on the B4145, which is named Thornton Road. Approached from Haworth, you need to head east out of the town and pick up the A629. Follow it in a southerly direction, through Denholme and taking a left turn onto the A644 for just a short distance. The B6145 takes you east into Thornton and keeping on this road for around two kilometres, you will see the church of St James on your left, along with the ruin of the Old Bell Chapel and graveyard on the right. It is usually possible to park on this wide road to visit the key sites of interest.

We suggest your first visit should be to the site of the Old Bell Chapel. Surrounded by the headstones of the graveyard, you can clearly see the footprint of the original chapel, a small section of which still stands. Information boards help you to understand the former layout along with a history of this location.

The Rev. Patrick Brontë was curate at this church from 1815, for five years, and it was here that all of his children, with the exception of their first born Maria, were baptised. Elizabeth, Charlotte, Branwell,

Emily and Anne are all listed in the register of baptisms which can be viewed across the road in St James Church. It is an interesting area to wander around and although close to the main road, quite tranquil amongst the mature trees. The chapel had an unusual octagonal bell tower which can be seen in old photographs taken prior to the 1870s, when the new Victorian St James's Church was opened opposite. The bell tower still stands in the grounds.

When Patrick Brontë arrived at his new ministry at Thornton he discovered that his church was in a very bad state of neglect. The church aisles were paved with wet gravestones, the windows were small and partly covered by two galleries and the whole interior was dark, damp and dismal. The south wall was actually crumbling and in danger of falling down. A recommendation from the Archdeacon in 1795 to repair the building had not been carried out.

Patrick Brontë, with his usual energy and vigour, immediately set about to make the place safe for the congregation and worthy of its role as a house of God. By the autumn of 1818, a new roof, windows and a west tower had been erected. Unfortunately, the chapel was still a dismal and gloomy place according to writers and visitors of the time who complained that the gravestone floor still emitted a foul smell and damp was prevalent. Pictures and photographs taken in the nineteenth century show a rather plain and unwelcoming building.

A chapel has been built and rebuilt on this site over the centuries and it is very difficult to know how each reconstruction looked, or whether it pleased and served the needs of the local people. Three stones set in the east wall record dates of 1587, 1612 and 1756. None are necessarily accurate but possibly record dates of alterations and rebuilding. There is evidence that suggests that a religious building possibly stood here in the twelfth century.

Today one sees a small, romantic ruin enveloped in its graveyard and a charming place to think about and remember its long history. Patrick Brontë preached from the high pulpit to a congregation that included his wife and young children.

Take some time to familiarise yourself with some of the interesting features of this ruin and the graves here. Note that the cupola is smaller than the square tower on which it sits; it may predate the tower, or it may have been brought here from another church. Very little is known for certain. It may be the original housing for the bell that now sits in St James's church and is dated 1664. Note around the outside of the east window the remains of three carved heads in a triangular configuration: one male and one female at each side and at the top, one of a child.

Like the chapel, the graveyard has been altered and extended over time and there are stones here from the seventeenth to the twentieth century. As with any graveyard be careful when stepping around the area. Vaults, crypts and holes are often hidden but, thanks to the hard work of the local community, this once sadly overgrown and neglected area is now a beautiful and peaceful cemetery.

Depending on the time of your visit, you can access St James's Church, (consecrated in 1872) and you will be able to view an exhibition of artefacts linked both to the Old Bell Chapel and to the Brontë family. This collection is a treasure of historical and religious interest and we urge you to spend time in this building viewing the excellent display and noting the features of this Victorian church.

The original font from the Bell Chapel, and used in the baptism of the Brontë children, is located on the north side, amongst the pews (do not be confused by the font that is still in use at the back of the church). This old stone font was probably made locally and is hand carved. It stands on a rough plinth and consists of an octagonal shaft and a decorative basin which is inscribed in Latin, 'AQUA PERFICIT ADLA VACRUM: ANNO: D 1679', translated as meaning that whoever passes through the waters is made perfect. The font stands 5ft high and was still in occasional use in the twentieth century.

A series of interesting and informative display boards guide you through the history of the Brontës' residence in this part of West Yorkshire, including copies of the baptisms records, along with a writing desk and other items of interest. Note especially the beautiful oak chest that formerly held the parochial records. A stand was made for it around 1730 as, presumably, the damp floors in the Bell Chapel were seeping into the wood and damaging the contents. The chest is inscribed, 'Ex Dono Tim Wadsworth de Brearley AD 1685'.

When you leave St James's church, turn right (west) onto Thornton Road and immediate right once again, to follow a footpath northward at the side of the church. This path takes you to Old Brontë Road. Turn left along this road, now forming part of a housing area though it was almost certainly the main road two centuries ago. Walking westerly, this becomes Market Street after a short distance and to the location of the former parsonage at number 74, on the right-hand side.

Currently housing a bistro and coffee house built out from the original building frontage, a large plaque confirms the historical significance of this unassuming property. Four of the Brontë children were born at this location: Charlotte in 1816, Branwell in 1817, Emily in 1818 and finally Anne in 1820. Inside the shop, customers can sit by the fireside where Maria Brontë nursed her babies two centuries ago.

To return to your start point by St James's Church, you can use Green Lane or Brontë Place to walk back on to Thornton Road and the short walk eastwards to your transport. Three interesting sites with very significant links to the Brontë family's five years' stay in this West Yorkshire town.

Fact File – Walk 19: Thornton town Trail

Start/Finish – Grid ref: SE 105 327

OS Maps: Explorer 288 (1:25,000), Landranger 104 (1:50,000)

Start/finish: St James's Church, Thornton Road, Thornton. 6km west of Bradford City centre, on B6145.

General Information – this is a short circular walk on paths around the town, with street parking available. Small number of shops, including coffee house at the Brontë's former home in Market Street.

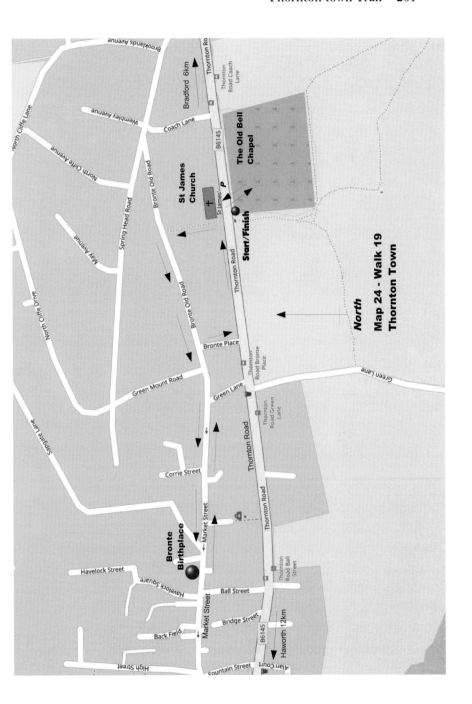

Map 24 - Walk 19
Thornton Town

North

The Old Bell Chapel

St James Church

Start/Finish

Bronte Birthplace

Above: The cupola of the original bell tower, which gave the chapel its name.

Below: Looking from the west towards the remaining ruin on the east side of the chapel. This chapel was originally built in 1612 but there has been a place of worship on this site for a very long time.

Above: Take a look inside the former tiny vestry and also note the outside of the east wall with its stone faces.

Right: The three stone tablets of various dates. They were located together during restoration and now cover a former window.

Above: A view of St. James' church, which was built in the 1870's, taken from the Old Bell Chapel grounds.

Left: There are some beautiful items of furniture from the Old Chapel, displayed here alongside some informative display boards describing the history of the Brontë family.

Right: This is the original font from the Bell Chapel in which the youngest five of the six Brontë children were all baptised.

Below: The Baptismal records on display in St James' church, showing the names of the Brontë siblings, Elizabeth, Charlotte and Patrick Branwell.

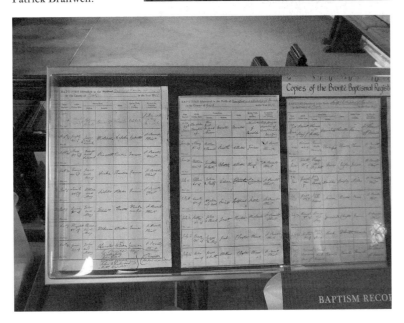

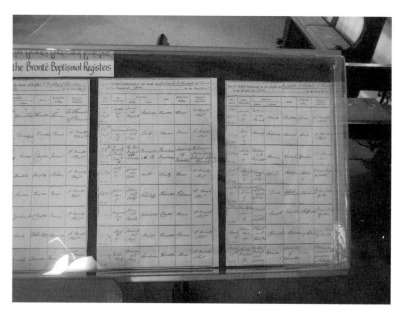

Above: The Baptismal records for Emily and Anne Brontë.

Below: The former rectory at 74 Market Street, Thornton where the Brontë family spent five years before moving to Haworth. It is currently an Italian Coffee Shop.

Above: The plaque on the house wall recording the births here of the four youngest Brontë children.

Right: The fireplace in the former parlour where Mrs Brontë nursed her babies.

Chapter 20

The art of walking and its effect on the Brontës

We decided to end this book with some information on walking and its necessity for people living in the nineteenth century and how it affected the lives, and possibly the deaths, of the Brontë siblings.

Walking is an art form. It can be one of the most healthy and pleasurable pastimes for people and animals alike. Walking can also be difficult, painful, tiring and a chore. Everything depends on the circumstances and the attitude of the individual.

Walking as a mode of travel was, for centuries, the only option for the vast majority of the pre-industrial population. As the nineteenth century advanced, new methods of transport were developed and dependency on walking, horseback or horse and carriage (which had been almost exclusively for the wealthy) was superseded firstly by rail and later by motor vehicles which could be enjoyed by all. This has meant that in the twenty-first century, walking has become far less of a necessity and, for some people, more of a pastime.

When the Brontës came to Haworth in 1820 almost everyone in the town walked wherever they wanted to go. Only a rich few had their own horses and carriages and public coaches were expensive for travellers. Therefore, walking was the only possibility for many and this included the Brontë family, for much of their lives.

Patrick Brontë's parish stretched over many miles but he did not own or keep a horse. He walked around all the neighbouring villages and he walked regularly, to Bradford, Leeds and Halifax, as did Branwell. A walk of thirty to fifty kilometres, (twenty to thirty miles) in a day was not unusual for men at this time and this was often over rough terrain with very poor roads and inadequate walking apparel. In 1832, Branwell paid a surprise visit to Charlotte whilst she was at Roe Head School. The round trip was over sixty-five kilometres (forty miles) and all done in a day. There were no strong leather walking boots or waterproof coats for most people, just wool cloaks and their daily shoes or clogs, or bare feet for the very poor. Everyone covered their heads winter and summer, the men in caps or hats and the ladies in bonnets and shawls. If people got wet it could take days to dry out their heavy clothes and would inhibit further travels. Chills, damp and moisture may also have exacerbated illness and people already weakened with age, poor diets and bad living conditions, will have suffered.

Women were not expected to go out unaccompanied and were seen as less robust and less capable than men. However, the Brontë siblings had a huge playground on their doorstep and ran and walked and played on the moors above their home from early childhood. Later the girls would walk together to Keighley or Stanbury, but would not trek enormous distances like the menfolk. They would all view walking as a necessary, though sometimes pleasurable and at other times hard and tedious, mode of travel.

Unfortunately, all the Brontë family were affected by weakness of the lungs and each of the six children died of the complications of tuberculosis. In their many letters, especially Charlotte's, they record constant coughs, colds, influenza, bronchitis, fever, lethargy, fatigue, weight loss, chills, loss of appetite and gastric upsets. Walking was both a cause of, and an antidote for, some of their symptoms.

Whilst the fresh and bracing air of the moors would have helped to keep them fit and healthy in good weather, the snow, rain, damp, fog and mists will have sapped their strength and further weakened their lungs. Tuberculosis is an illness that once contracted can lay dormant for many months, even years, and then flare up to give painful and debilitating symptoms before a final, fatal attack.

Charlotte and Anne write of the biting east wind in spring that often kept them indoors and ill for days on end. Heavy snow and driving rain in the winter months kept them all housebound in cold rooms with unlit fires. By necessity the windows remained shut to keep the house warmer, but this meant a lack of healthy ventilation. The stone floors of the Parsonage and the lack of fires and warmth would affect their health and prevent a quick recovery from persistent coughs and colds. The drying and airing of damp clothes and bedding would further affect the family.

Patrick Brontë complained for many years of bronchial troubles and wore a high, wound cloth around his neck to help keep out chills and protect his throat and lungs. Maria and Elizabeth Brontë both died in childhood after experiencing the 'low fever' at their school and succumbing to tuberculosis some weeks later. Branwell was ill for the last few years of his life with constant debilitation, fatigue, cough and loss of appetite. This was partly due to his misuse of alcohol but he too died of 'Chronic Bronchitis-Marasmus' according to Dr Wheelhouse and it was probably the same consumption, or tuberculosis, that was rife both in the village and in his own family.

Emily was said to have caught a cold at Branwell's funeral and never left the house again. She died of tuberculosis twelve weeks later. Anne had asthma for most of her life and in her last months she too was diagnosed with tuberculosis. In an attempt to improve her health she travelled to Scarborough, with Charlotte and Ellen Nussey, hoping that the sea air would prolong her life. Unfortunately, she died within a few days.

Charlotte contracted a heavy cold after a walk to the 'Brontë' waterfall with her new husband when they were caught in a rainstorm. This and early pregnancy debilitated her enough for the dormant tuberculosis to cause her death a few weeks later.

The story of the Brontë siblings is very neatly summed up in one of Charlotte's poems, 'Retrospection'. In these three short verses she celebrates the blessings of childhood when they all worked and played together and nurtured their love of reading and writing.

She describes how in their teenage years they strove forward with enthusiasm cutting their way through life, but she then starts to question their efforts and expectations. She moves on to state how quickly and inevitably life comes to an end and she wonders whether all their struggles were for nothing. She wrote,

We wove a web in childhood,
A web of sunny air;
We dug a spring in infancy
Of water pure and fair;

We sowed in youth a mustard seed,
We cut an almond rod;
We are now grown up to riper age:
Are they withered in the sod?

Are they blighted, failed and faded,
Are they mouldered back to clay?
For life is darkly shaded,
And its joys fleet fast away!

Charlotte Brontë. December 1835

Nowadays, the majority of us walk as much for pleasure as necessity and we tend to do so when we find the weather agreeable to our needs. We have multiple alternatives of both transport and communication; the internet and the telephone have allowed us to order goods, to find information and to talk to friends and family, without the need to physically move ourselves to their location.

However, the benefits of walking in this century are manifold and whilst we have the ability, the space and the suitable clothing, we should all walk as much as possible. Walking can assist both our mental and physical health. Mentally, it can improve confidence, memory, learning, concentration and reasoning and may also help to offset the beginnings of dementia. Physically, walking can energise the body and reduce stress, it helps with weight control and reduces cholesterol. It can stave off diabetes, strokes, heart disease and high blood pressure. It increases bone health and density and lowers the incidence of osteoporosis.

Awareness of the benefits of walking and the pleasure it can give when taken in the countryside, or as part of a wander around a new town or place of interest, adds to the enjoyment. We have tried in this book to show you some beautiful walks, some interesting places, and a description of the life and times of a literary family who happened to live in Haworth at a time of great change. We hope you understand a little more about how the advent of the industrial age affected Yorkshire and its people. You can still find many open spaces and exhilarating walks amongst the towns, villages, hills and countryside of this varied and often beautiful county, which is so rich in social and industrial history, art and literature.

The contrast of the past and the present, are demonstrated in the last two photographs of this book, on the page opposite. Mill chimneys once dominated the skyline of every big town and city, especially the northern mill towns of Lancashire and Yorkshire. The noise, smoke and dirt that they produced polluted the neighbourhood and affected the health of the community. They did, however, supply thousands of jobs for the growing population. Very few remain as symbols to the past.

Today steam and coal have been superseded by oil, electricity, nuclear power and, more recently, solar energy, and wind turbines with their more ecologically friendly blades generating invisible electricity. As we move forward in our now digital age, pollution comes in other forms and guises but power and energy, in whatever mode, will always be needed.

It is important to remember the old ways and the people of the past and the efforts they made to improve and enhance society, so

that in the 21st century people in this country, and many others, can live healthier, easier and more entertaining lives. There is still much evidence of the past remaining which can help modern society to recall and appreciate its heritage.

Haworth and its surrounding area, holds a unique and vital place in the history of northern England and the industrial revolution. The Brontë family were a product of this environment and they described its attractions and hardships with eloquence and sensitivity. The places that they knew and loved have held on to much of their history and beauty. Today, we can have the pleasure of walking through this Yorkshire landscape whilst appreciating the lives and times of all those who walked this way before us.

Bibliography

Alexander, C. and Pearson S. L. *Celebrating Charlotte Brontë: Transforming Life into Literature* The Brontë Society, Haworth 2016.

Atkinson, E. (Ed) *Haworth in the Brontë Era: B. H. Babbage's visit to Haworth* Fretwell Publishing, Keighley 1998. (Pamphlet)

Bairstow, J. M. *The Railways of Keighley* Dalesman Books, Yorkshire 1979.

Barker, J. R. V. *The Brontës* (Revised Edition), Abacus, London 2010.

Barker, J. R. V. *The Brontës Selected Poems* Everyman Classic, Guernsey Press, 1985.

Baumer, M. *A History of Haworth from Earliest Times* Carnegie Publishing Ltd. Lancaster, 2009.

Brontë, C. *Jane Eyre* Norton and Company, Inc, New York, 1971.

Brontë, C. *Shirley* Penguin English Library, Middlesex, 1974.

Brontë, E. J. *Wuthering Heights* Penguin Classics, London, 2011.

Craven, J. *A Brontë Moorland Village and its People: A History of Stanbury* Rydal Press, Keighley, 1907.

Dewhirst, I. *A History of Keighley* (Revised Edition) Tempus Publishing Ltd, Gloucestershire, 2006.

Haigh, A. *Railways in West Yorkshire* Dalesman Books, Yorkshire, 1974.

Hatfield, C. W. *The Complete Poems of Emily Jane Brontë* Open University Press, London, 1941.

Kellett, J. *Haworth Parsonage – The Home of the Brontës* The Brontë Society, Yorkshire, 1977.

Lister, P. *Ghosts and Gravestones of Haworth* Tempus Publishing, Gloucestershire, 2006.

Riley, D. *Rise and Fall of Methodism in the Upper Worth Valley, Yorkshire, 1740–2013* Self-Publication, 2013.

Southwart, E. and Mackenzie, T. *Brontë Moors and Villages from Thornton to Haworth* The Bodley Head Ltd, London, 1923.

Turner, W. *A Spring-time Saunter. Round and About Brontë-land* The Amethyst Press, (Republished) 1984.

Ward, M. G. and Dinsdale, A. *A Guide to Historic Haworth and the Brontës* Mulberry Books, Keighley, 2000.

Whitehead, S. R. *The Brontës Haworth: The Place and the People the Brontës Knew* Ashmount Press, Haworth, 2006.

Whitworth, A. *The Old Bell Chapel, Thornton – A Brief History of the Chapel of St James.* Culva House Publications, Whitby. 2nd Edition, 2005.

Wood, S. and Brears, P. *The Real Wuthering Heights – The Story of the Withins Farms.* Amberley Publishing, Gloucestershire, 2016.

Wood, S. *Haworth – "A strange uncivilised little place"* The History Press, Gloucestershire, Reprinted and Revised, 2012.

Wood, S. *Haworth, Oxenhope and Stanbury from Old Photographs. – Volume One, Domestic and Social Life.* Amberley Publishing, Gloucestershire, 2011.

Wood, S. *Haworth, Oxenhope and Stanbury from Old Photographs – Volume Two, Trade and Industry.* Amberley Publishing, Gloucestershire, 2011

Websites

Open Street Maps. www.openstreetmaps.org/